KU-543-915

Please return / renew by date shown.
You can renew it at:
norlink.norfolk.gov.uk
or by telephone: 0344 800 8006
Please have your library card & PIN ready

NORFOLK COUNTY LIBRARY
WITHDRAWN FOR SALE

NORFOLK LIBRARY
AND INFORMATION SERVICE

DESIGNER **KRYSTAL HENNES**

ASSISTANT EDITOR **FREDDYE LINS**

EDITOR **RANDY STRADLEY**

PUBLISHER **MIKE RICHARDSON**

Special thanks to Joanne Chan Taylor, Leland Chee, Troy Alders, Carol Roeder, Jann Moorhead, and David Anderman at Lucas Licensing.

Published by Dark Horse Books, a division of Dark Horse Comics, Inc.
10956 SE Main Street, Milwaukie, OR 97222

DarkHorse.com | StarWars.com

To find a comics shop in your area, call the Comic Shop Locator Service toll-free at 1.888.266.4226
First edition: August 2012 | ISBN 978-1-59582-949-8

10 9 8 7 6 5 4 3 2 1

PRINTED AT 1010 PRINTING INTERNATIONAL, LTD., GUANGDONG PROVINCE, CHINA

Library of Congress Cataloging-in-Publication Data

Gilroy, Henry.
Star wars the clone wars : the Sith hunters / script, Henry Gilroy, Steven Melching ; pencils, Vicenc Villagrasa ; inks, Vicente Ibanez ; lettering, Michael Heisler ; cover art, Dave Filoni.
     p. cm.
Summary: "Darth Maul and his brother Savage Opress are loose in the galaxy. The Jedi Council sends a task force of Jedi to bring them to justice"--Provided by publisher.
ISBN 978-1-59582-949-8
1. Graphic novels. I. Melching, Steven. II. Filoni, Dave, ill. III. Star wars, the clone wars (Television program) IV. Title. V. Title: Sith hunters.
PZ7.7.G55Stm 2012
741.5'973--dc23
                          2012015596

STAR WARS: THE CLONE WARS—THE SITH HUNTERS

STAR WARS®

THE CLONE WARS™

THE SITH HUNTERS

SCRIPT **HENRY GILROY**
STEVEN MELCHING

INKS **VICENTE IBAÑEZ**

COLORS **MARLON ILAGAN**

PENCILS **VICENÇ VILLAGRASA**

LETTERING **MICHAEL HEISLER**

COVER ART **DAVE FILONI**

DARK HORSE BOOKS

LUCAS BOOKS

This story takes place shortly after the events in "Revenge," episode 22 of season 4 of *The Clone Wars*.

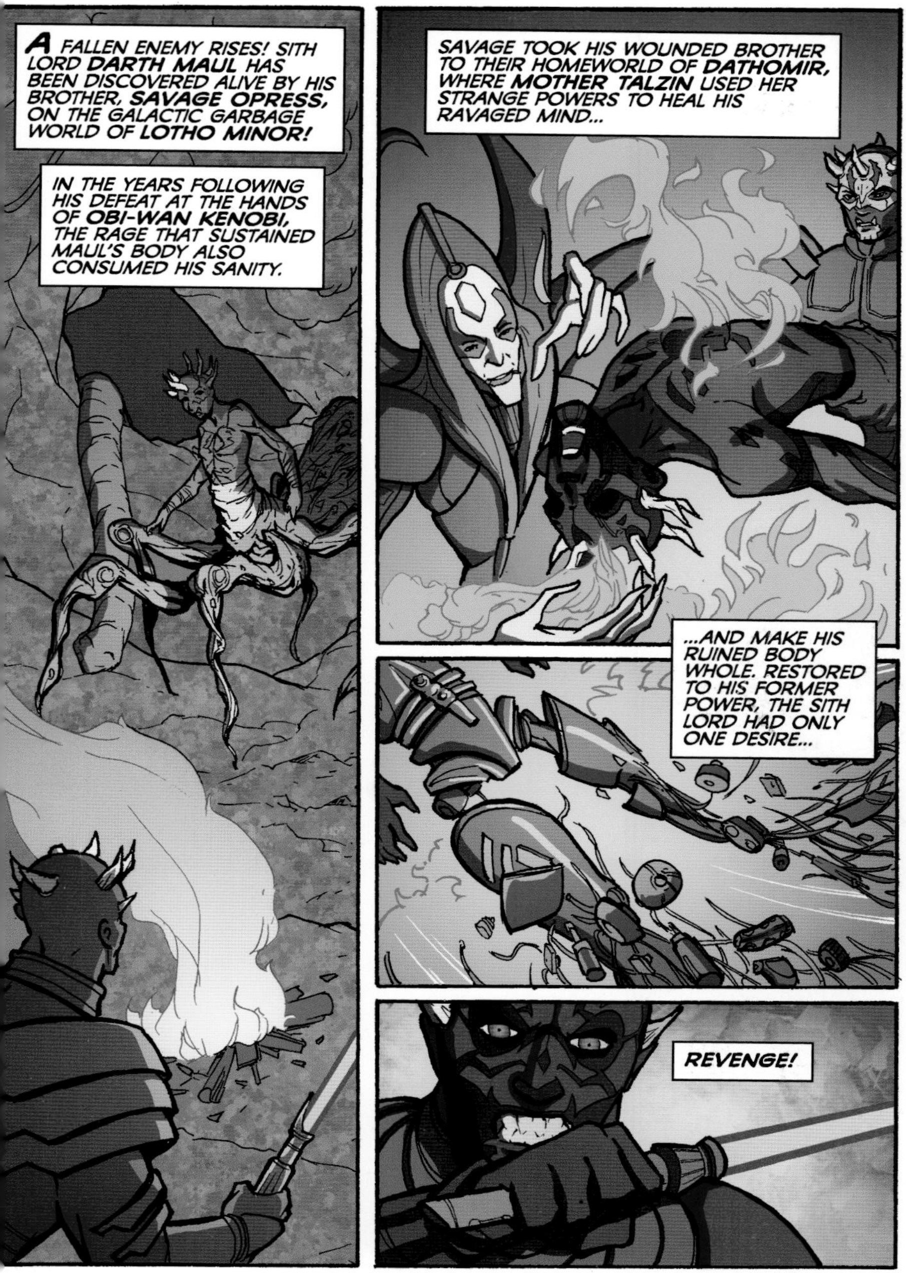
A FALLEN ENEMY RISES! SITH LORD DARTH MAUL HAS BEEN DISCOVERED ALIVE BY HIS BROTHER, SAVAGE OPRESS, ON THE GALACTIC GARBAGE WORLD OF LOTHO MINOR!
IN THE YEARS FOLLOWING HIS DEFEAT AT THE HANDS OF OBI-WAN KENOBI, THE RAGE THAT SUSTAINED MAUL'S BODY ALSO CONSUMED HIS SANITY.
SAVAGE TOOK HIS WOUNDED BROTHER TO THEIR HOMEWORLD OF DATHOMIR, WHERE MOTHER TALZIN USED HER STRANGE POWERS TO HEAL HIS RAVAGED MIND...
...AND MAKE HIS RUINED BODY WHOLE. RESTORED TO HIS FORMER POWER, THE SITH LORD HAD ONLY ONE DESIRE...
REVENGE!

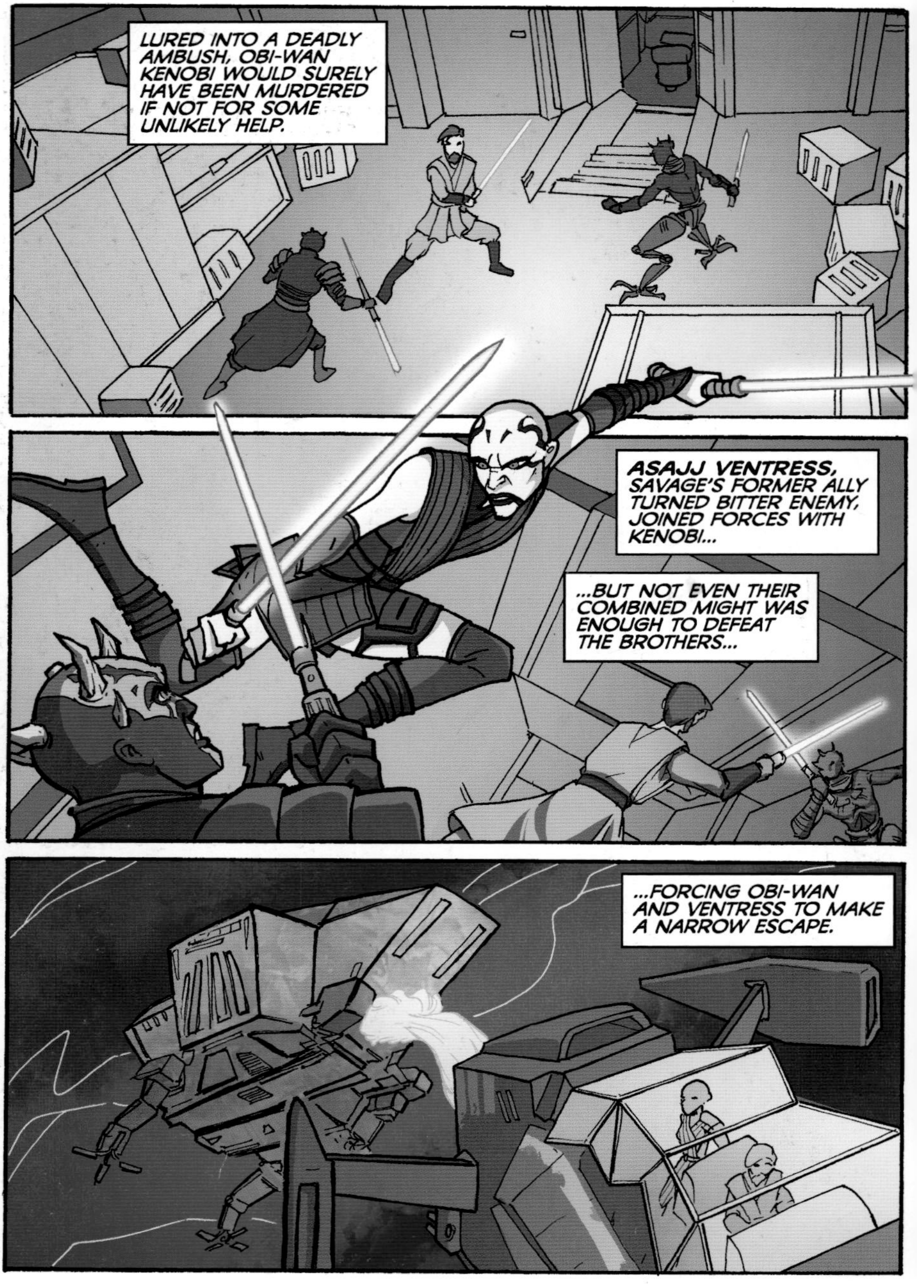
LURED INTO A DEADLY AMBUSH, OBI-WAN KENOBI WOULD SURELY HAVE BEEN MURDERED IF NOT FOR SOME UNLIKELY HELP.
ASAJJ VENTRESS, SAVAGE'S FORMER ALLY TURNED BITTER ENEMY, JOINED FORCES WITH KENOBI...
...BUT NOT EVEN THEIR COMBINED MIGHT WAS ENOUGH TO DEFEAT THE BROTHERS...
...FORCING OBI-WAN AND VENTRESS TO MAKE A NARROW ESCAPE.

WELL, WE'VE
ARRIVED, MY
DARLING...

ONE MUST TRY. IF
YOU COOPERATE WITH
THE JEDI AGAINST THE
SEPARATISTS, I WILL OFFER
FAVORABLE TESTIMONY AT
YOUR TRIAL. IT'S NOT
TOO LATE TO CHANGE
SIDES.

YOUR
SENTIMENTAL
NATURE WILL BE
YOUR DOOM,
KENOBI.

THE
ONLY *"SIDE"* I
CARE ABOUT IS
MY OWN.

GENERAL!

7

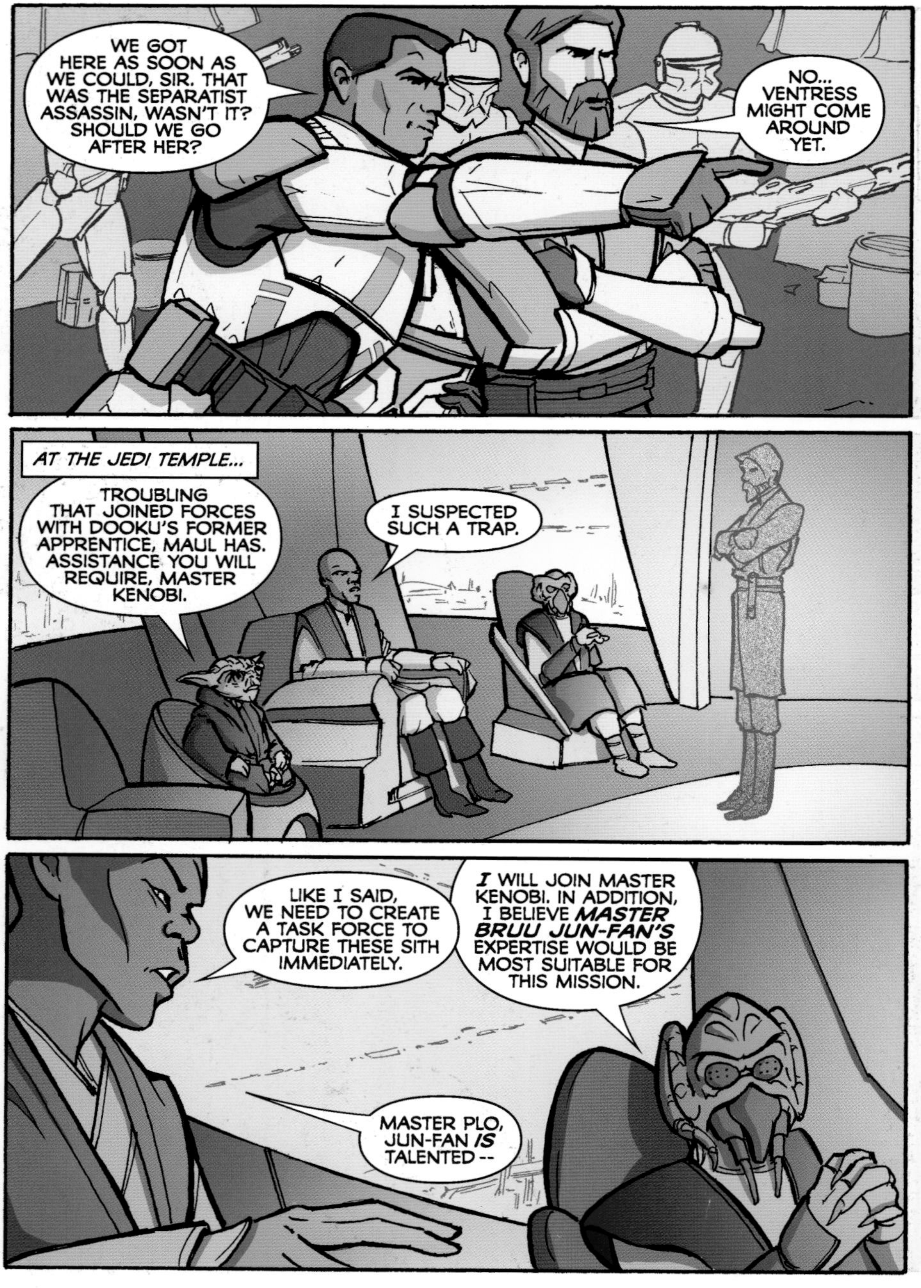
WE GOT HERE AS SOON AS WE COULD, SIR. THAT WAS THE SEPARATIST ASSASSIN, WASN'T IT? SHOULD WE GO AFTER HER?
NO... VENTRESS MIGHT COME AROUND YET.
AT THE JEDI TEMPLE...
TROUBLING THAT JOINED FORCES WITH DOOKU'S FORMER APPRENTICE, MAUL HAS. ASSISTANCE YOU WILL REQUIRE, MASTER KENOBI.
I SUSPECTED SUCH A TRAP.
LIKE I SAID, WE NEED TO CREATE A TASK FORCE TO CAPTURE THESE SITH IMMEDIATELY.
I WILL JOIN MASTER KENOBI. IN ADDITION, I BELIEVE MASTER BRUU JUN-FAN'S EXPERTISE WOULD BE MOST SUITABLE FOR THIS MISSION.
MASTER PLO, JUN-FAN IS TALENTED --

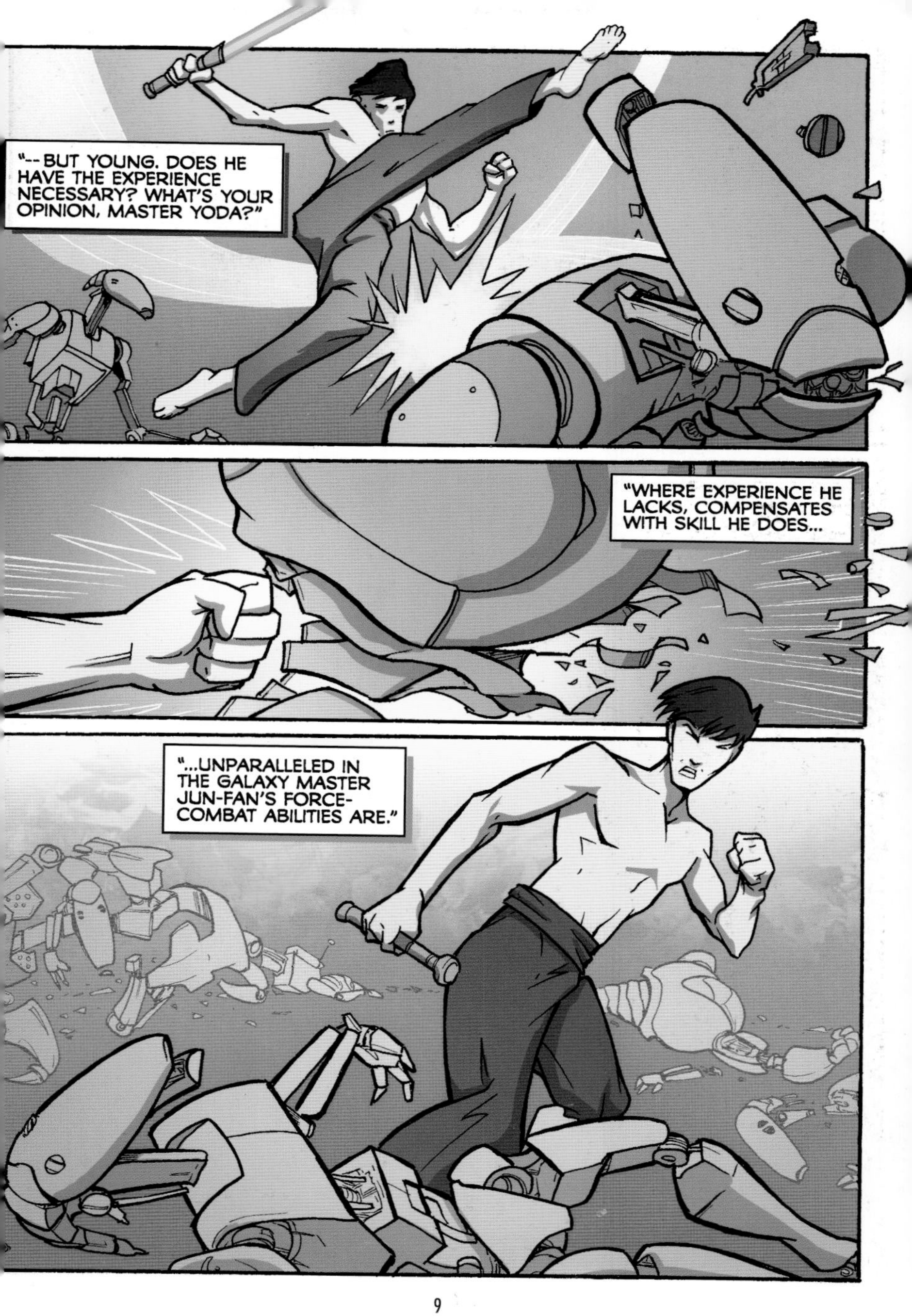
"-- BUT YOUNG. DOES HE HAVE THE EXPERIENCE NECESSARY? WHAT'S YOUR OPINION, MASTER YODA?"
"WHERE EXPERIENCE HE LACKS, COMPENSATES WITH SKILL HE DOES...
"...UNPARALLELED IN THE GALAXY MASTER JUN-FAN'S FORCE-COMBAT ABILITIES ARE."

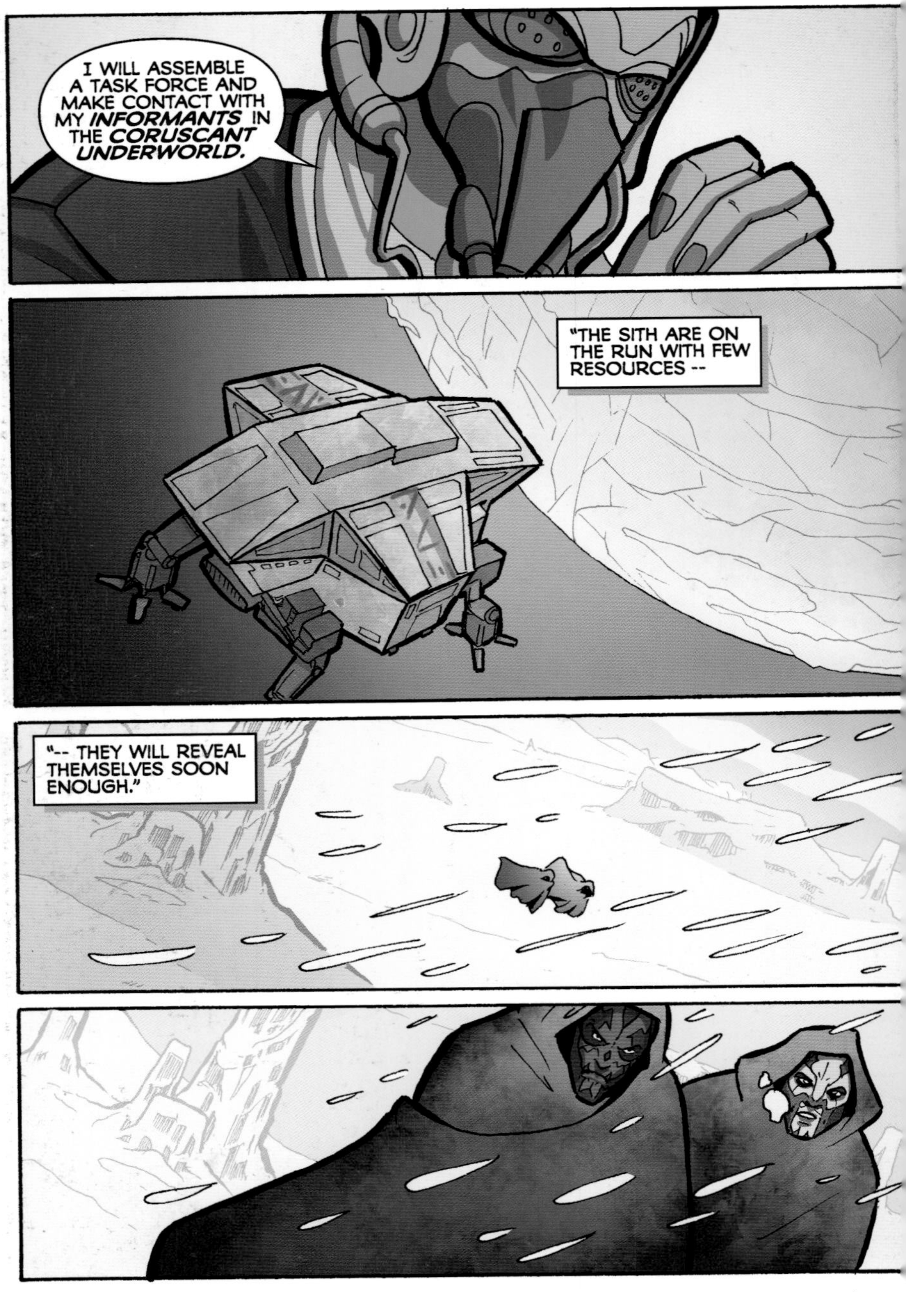
I WILL ASSEMBLE A TASK FORCE AND MAKE CONTACT WITH MY *INFORMANTS* IN THE *CORUSCANT UNDERWORLD.*
"THE SITH ARE ON THE RUN WITH FEW RESOURCES --
"-- THEY WILL REVEAL THEMSELVES SOON ENOUGH."

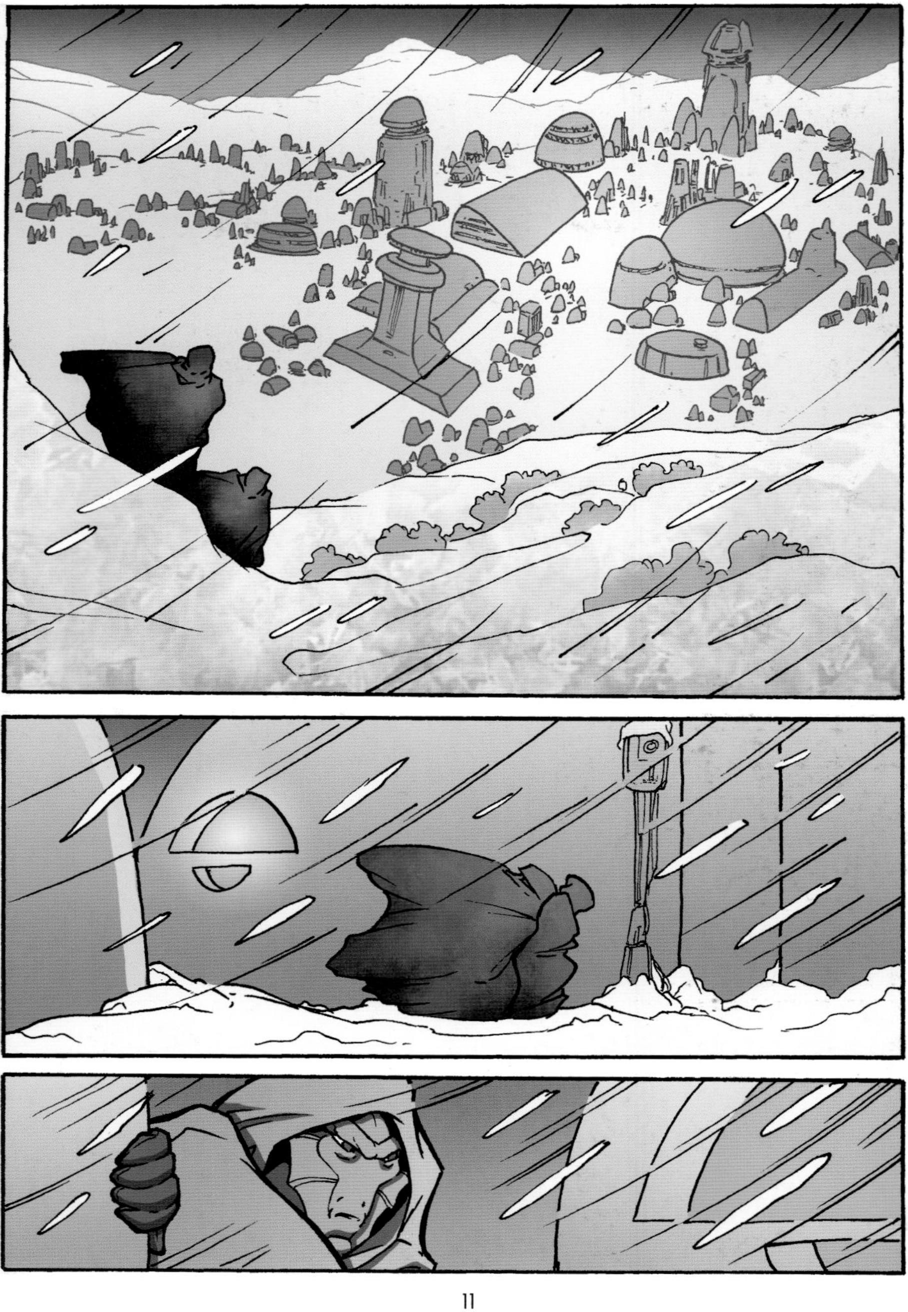

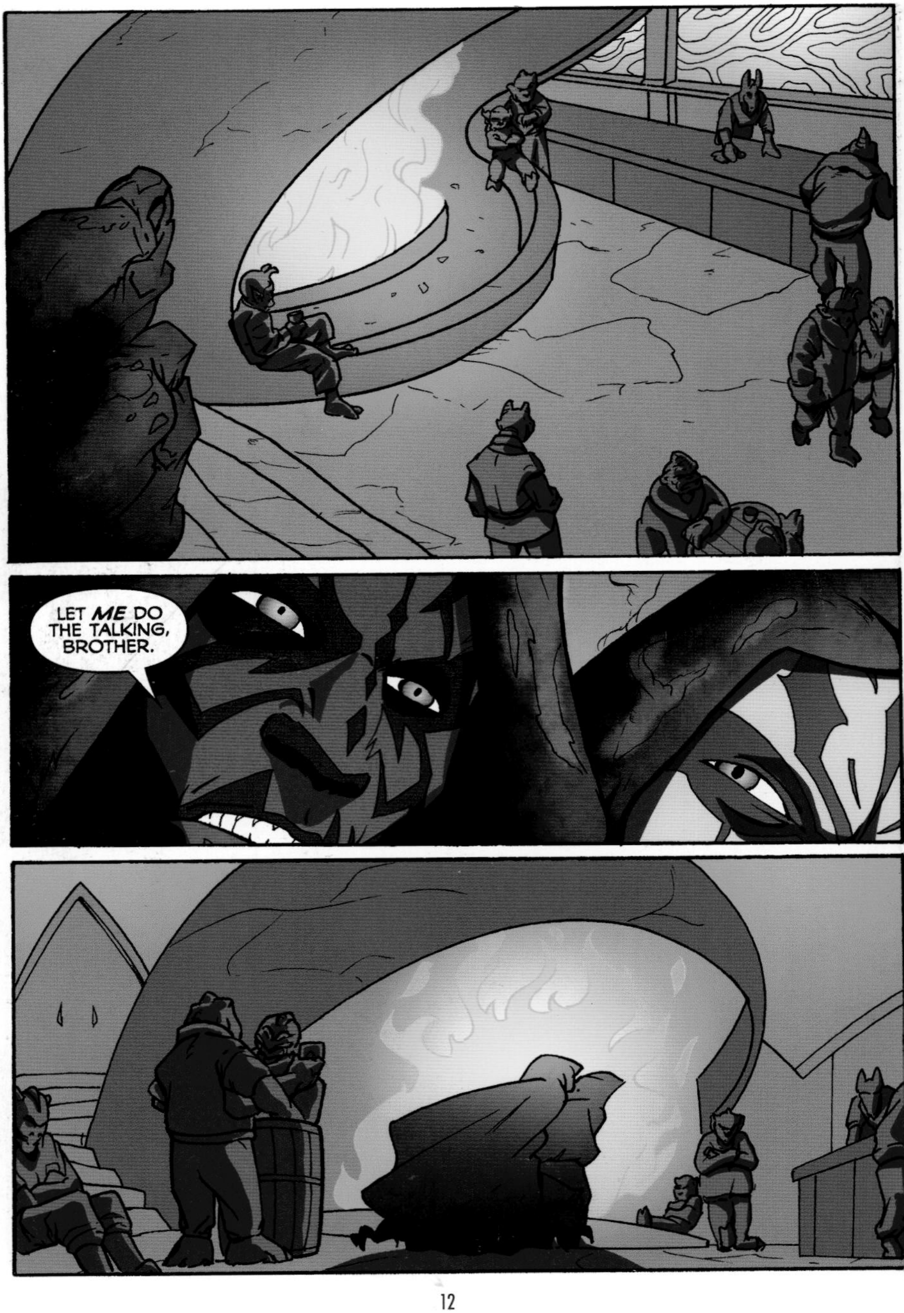
LET ME DO THE TALKING, BROTHER.

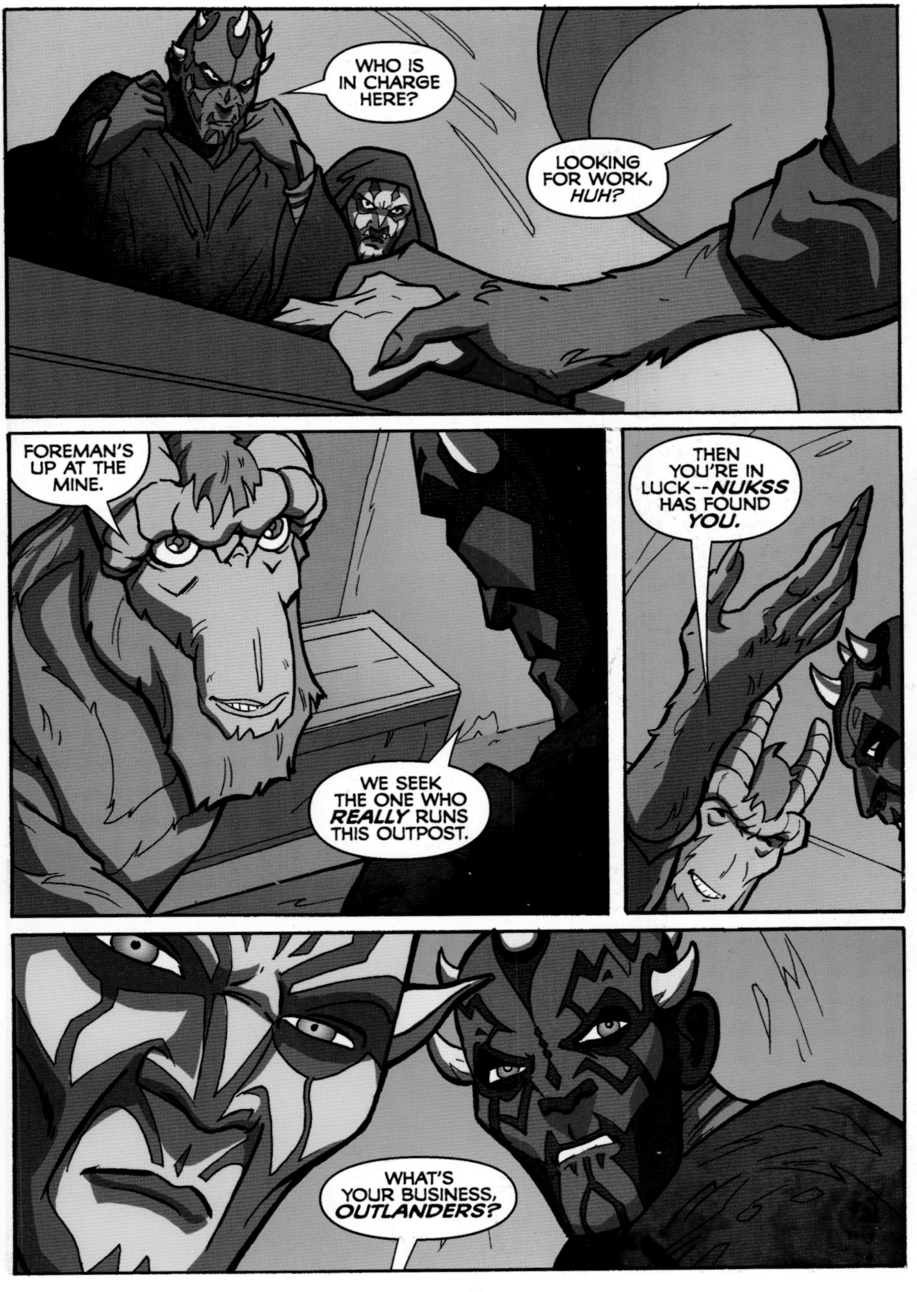
WHO IS IN CHARGE HERE?
LOOKING FOR WORK, *HUH?*
FOREMAN'S UP AT THE MINE.
WE SEEK THE ONE WHO *REALLY* RUNS THIS OUTPOST.
THEN YOU'RE IN LUCK--***NUKSS*** HAS FOUND ***YOU.***
WHAT'S YOUR BUSINESS, ***OUTLANDERS?***

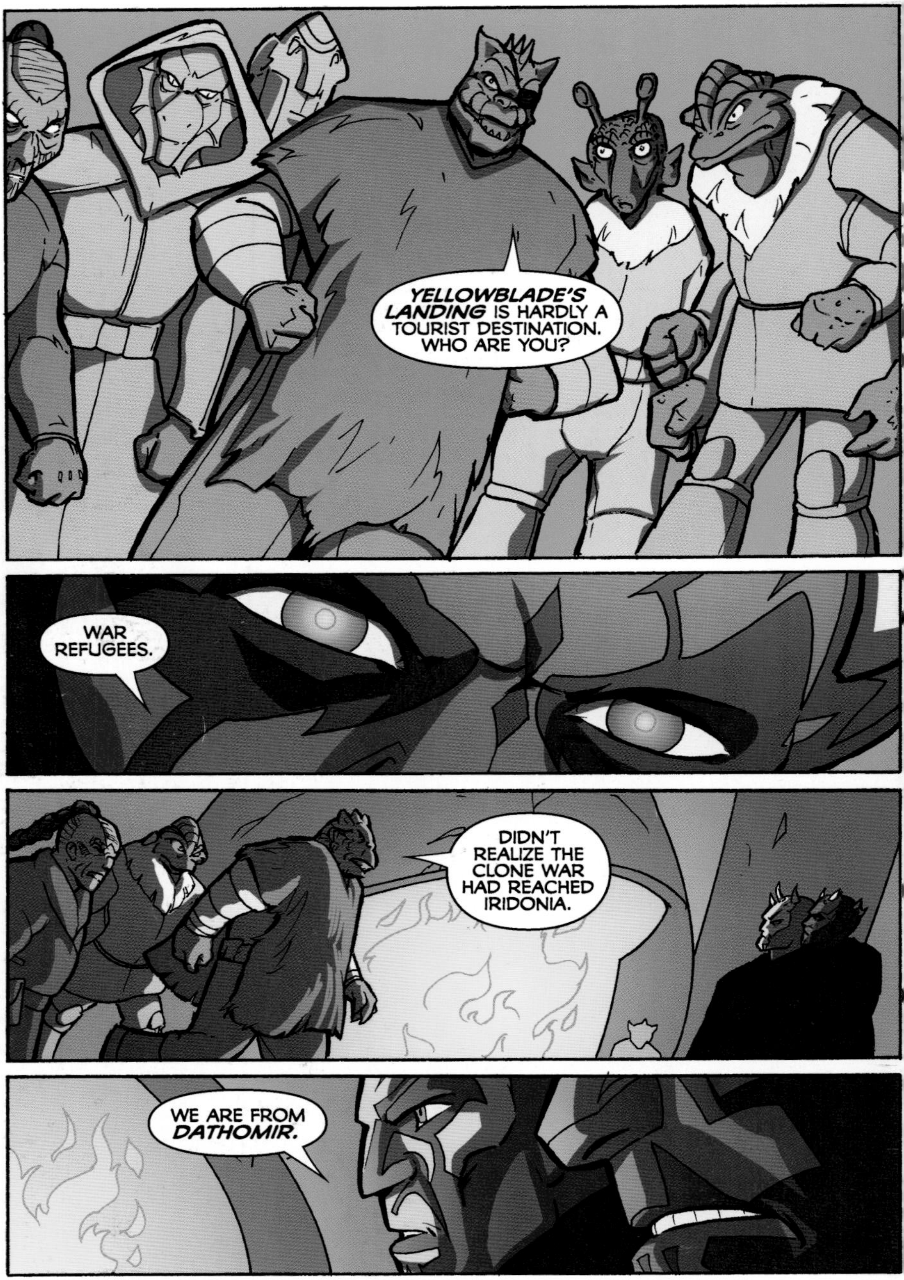
YELLOWBLADE'S LANDING IS HARDLY A TOURIST DESTINATION. WHO ARE YOU?
WAR REFUGEES.
DIDN'T REALIZE THE CLONE WAR HAD REACHED IRIDONIA.
WE ARE FROM DATHOMIR.

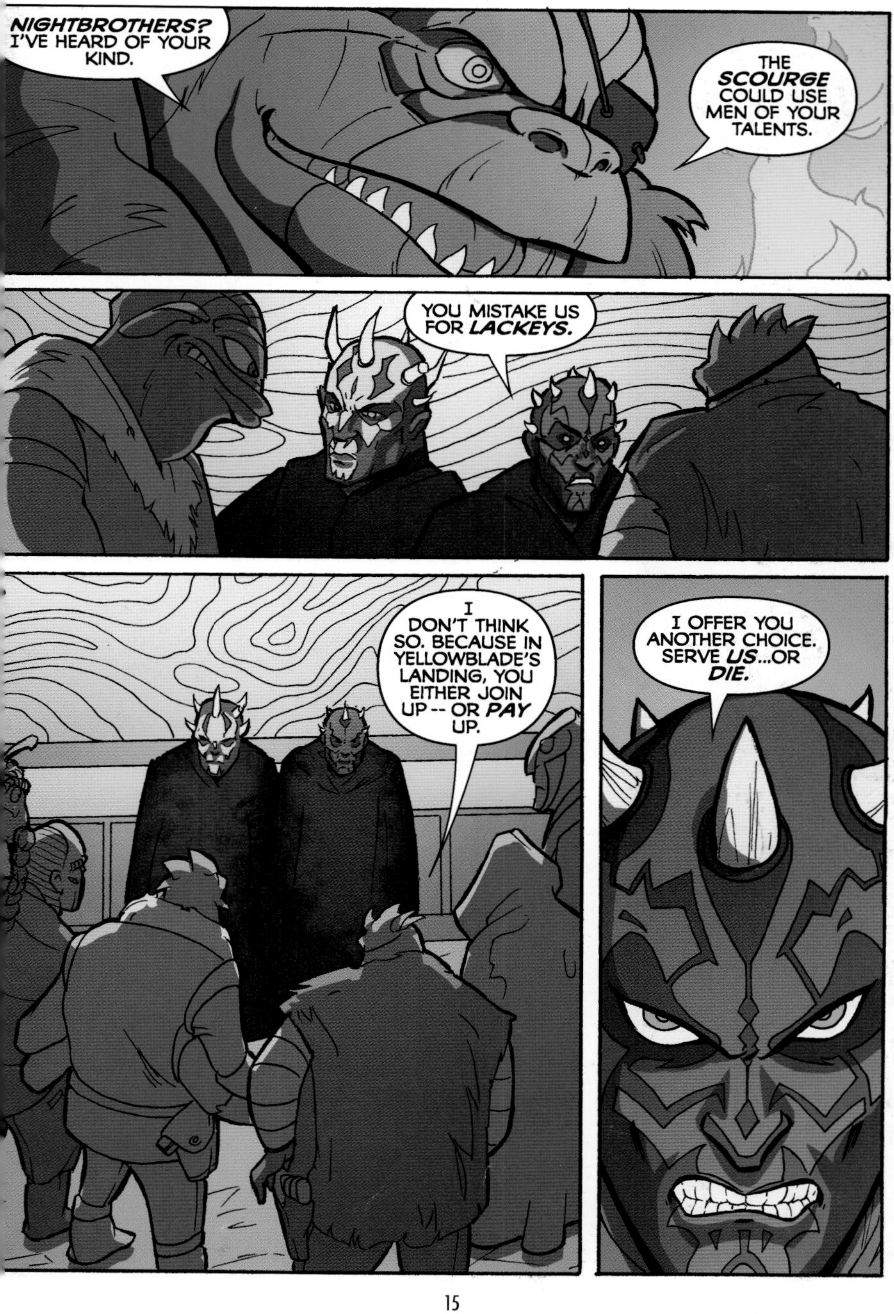
NIGHTBROTHERS? I'VE HEARD OF YOUR KIND.
THE SCOURGE COULD USE MEN OF YOUR TALENTS.
YOU MISTAKE US FOR LACKEYS.
I DON'T THINK SO. BECAUSE IN YELLOWBLADE'S LANDING, YOU EITHER JOIN UP -- OR PAY UP.
I OFFER YOU ANOTHER CHOICE. SERVE US...OR DIE.

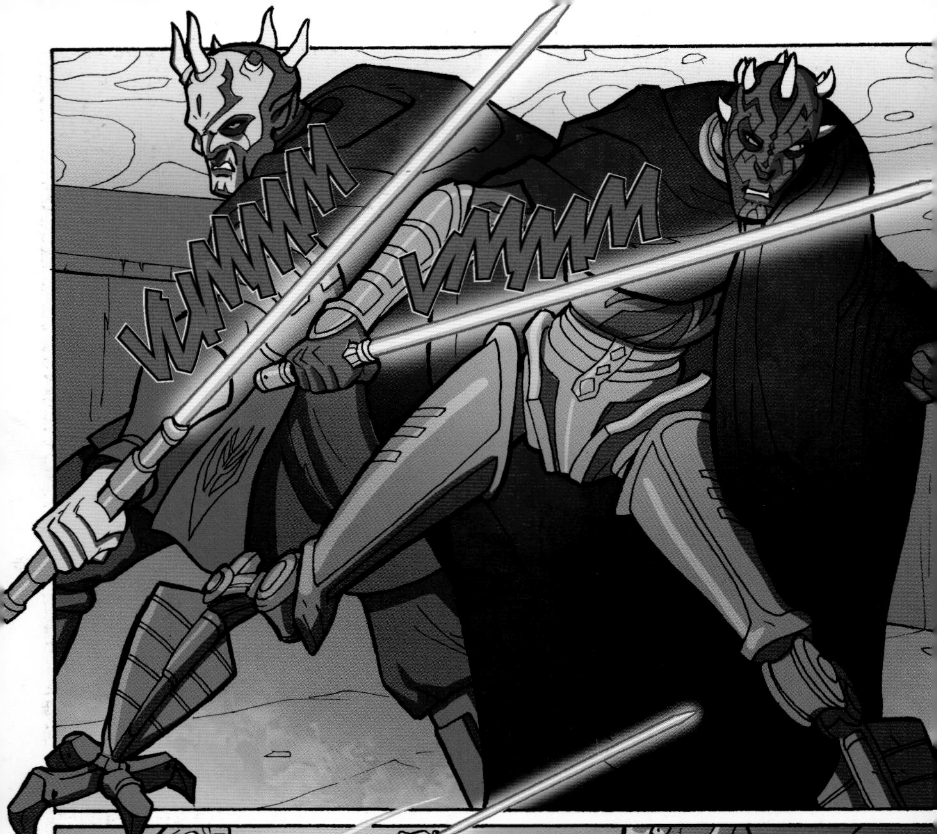
VVMMM
VVMMMM

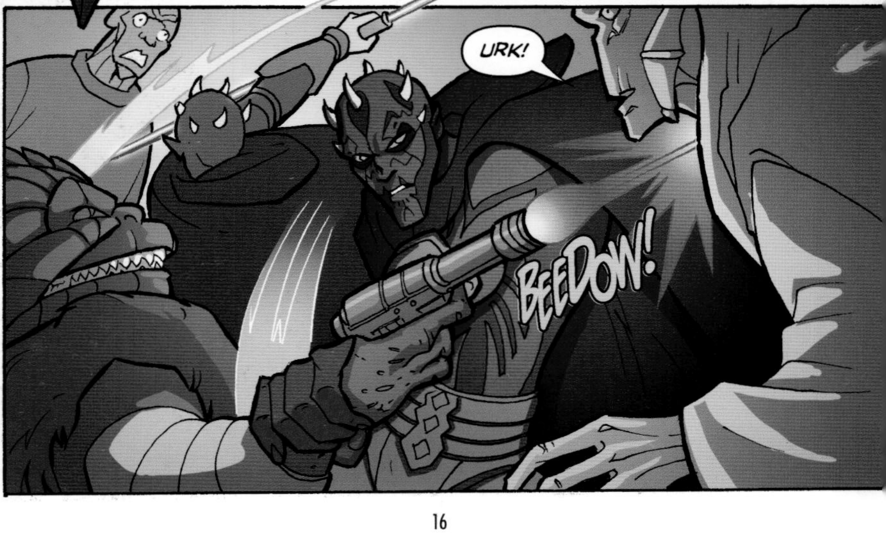
URK!
BEEDOW!

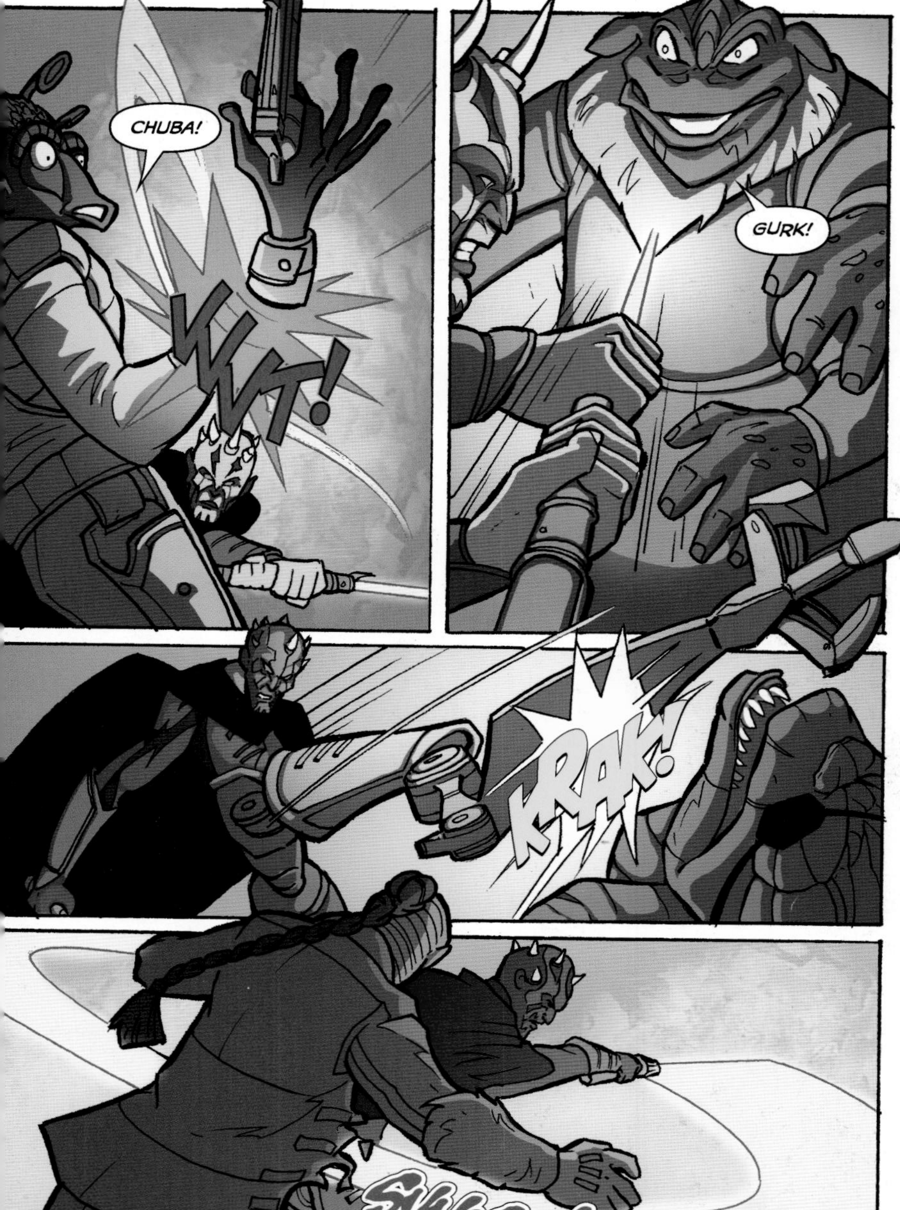
CHUBA!
VVVT!
GURK!
KRAK!
SWISH!

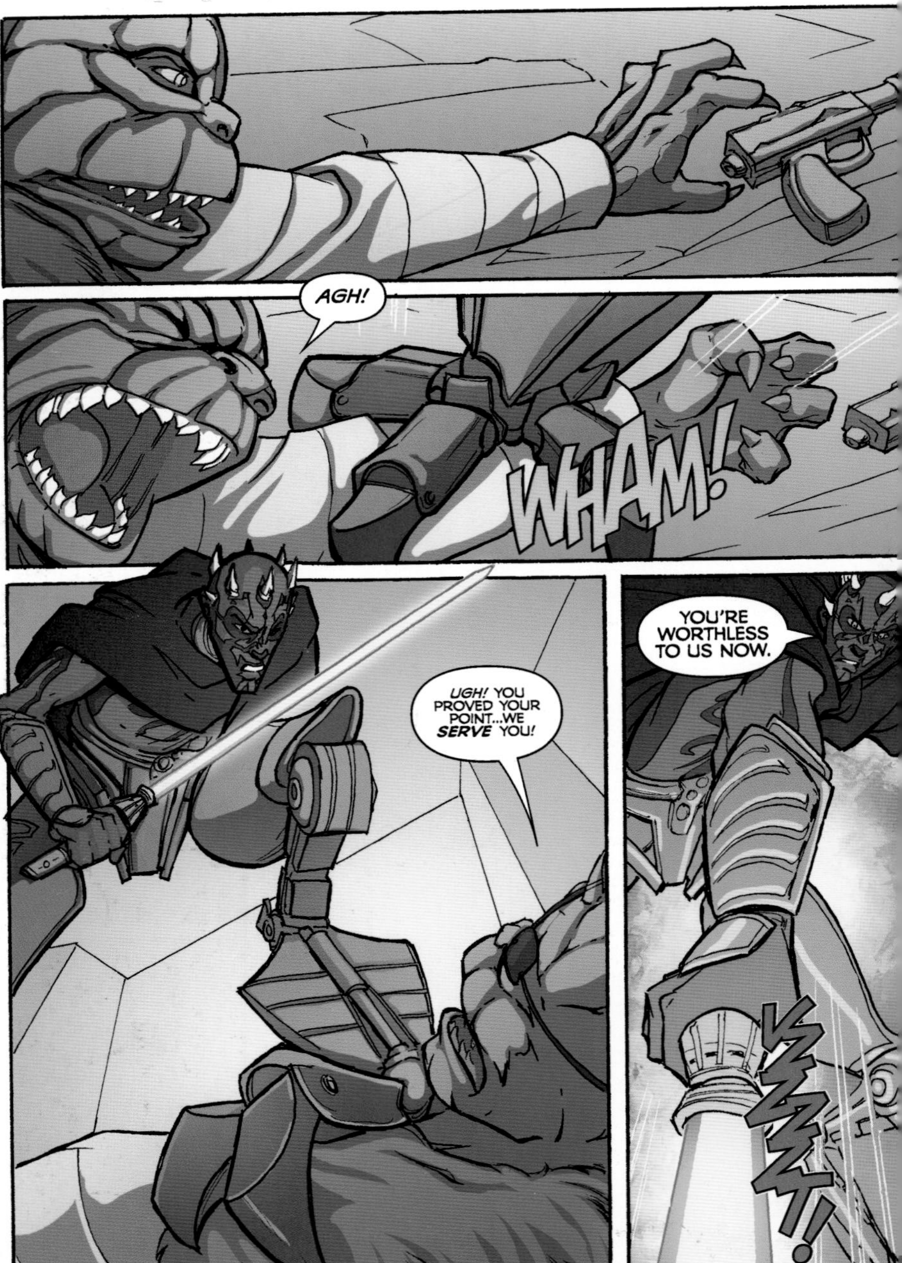
AGH!
WHAM!
UGH! YOU PROVED YOUR POINT...WE SERVE YOU!
YOU'RE WORTHLESS TO US NOW.
VWWWM!

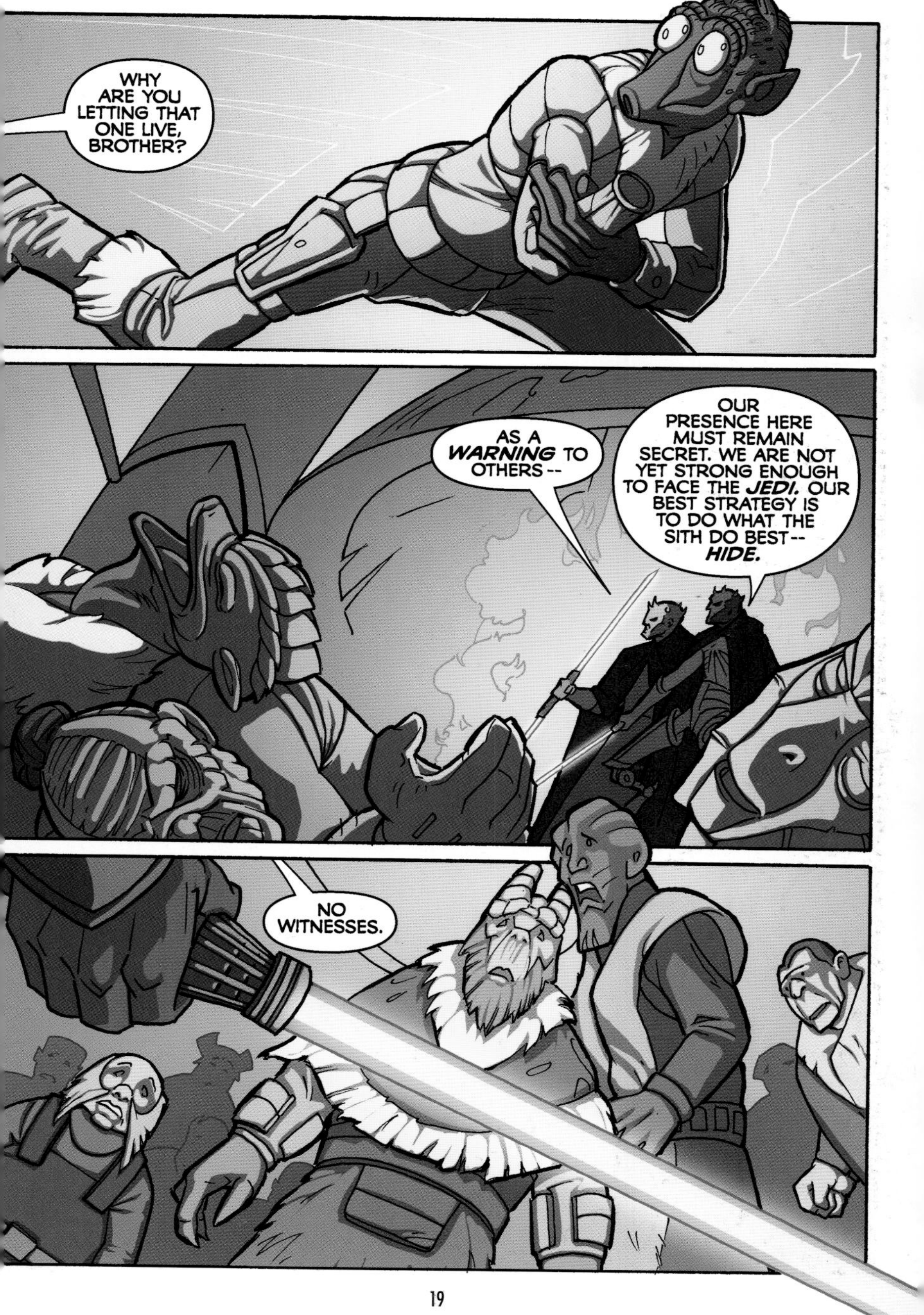
WHY ARE YOU LETTING THAT ONE LIVE, BROTHER?
AS A *WARNING* TO OTHERS--
OUR PRESENCE HERE MUST REMAIN SECRET. WE ARE NOT YET STRONG ENOUGH TO FACE THE *JEDI.* OUR BEST STRATEGY IS TO DO WHAT THE SITH DO BEST-- *HIDE.*
NO WITNESSES.

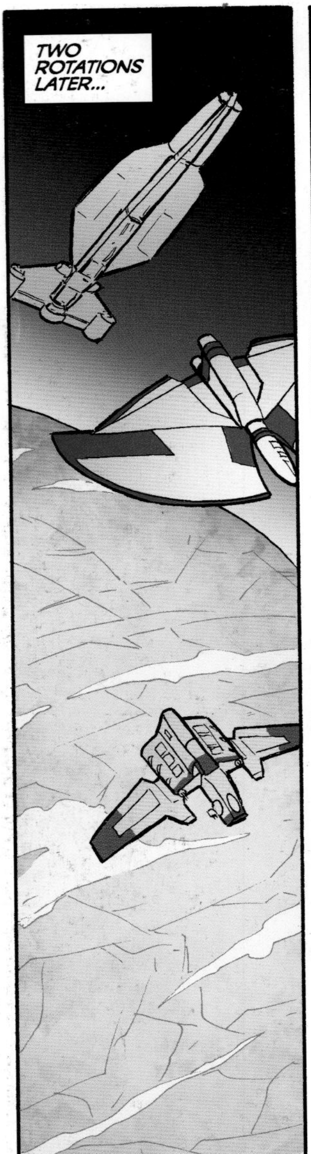
TWO ROTATIONS LATER...

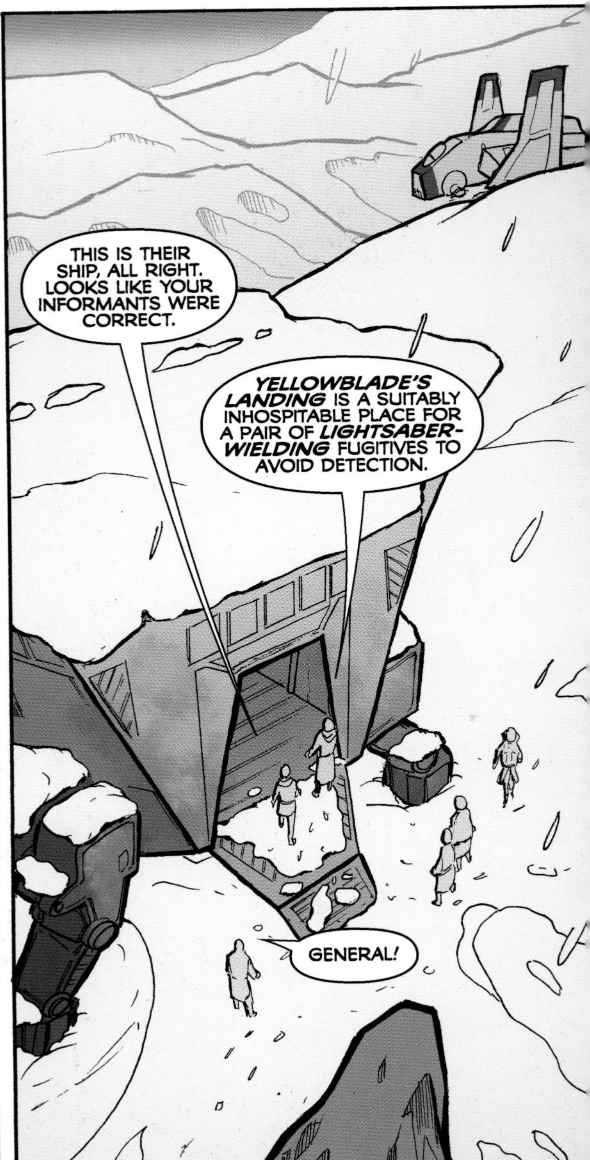
THIS IS THEIR SHIP, ALL RIGHT. LOOKS LIKE YOUR INFORMANTS WERE CORRECT.
YELLOWBLADE'S LANDING IS A SUITABLY INHOSPITABLE PLACE FOR A PAIR OF LIGHTSABER-WIELDING FUGITIVES TO AVOID DETECTION.
GENERAL!

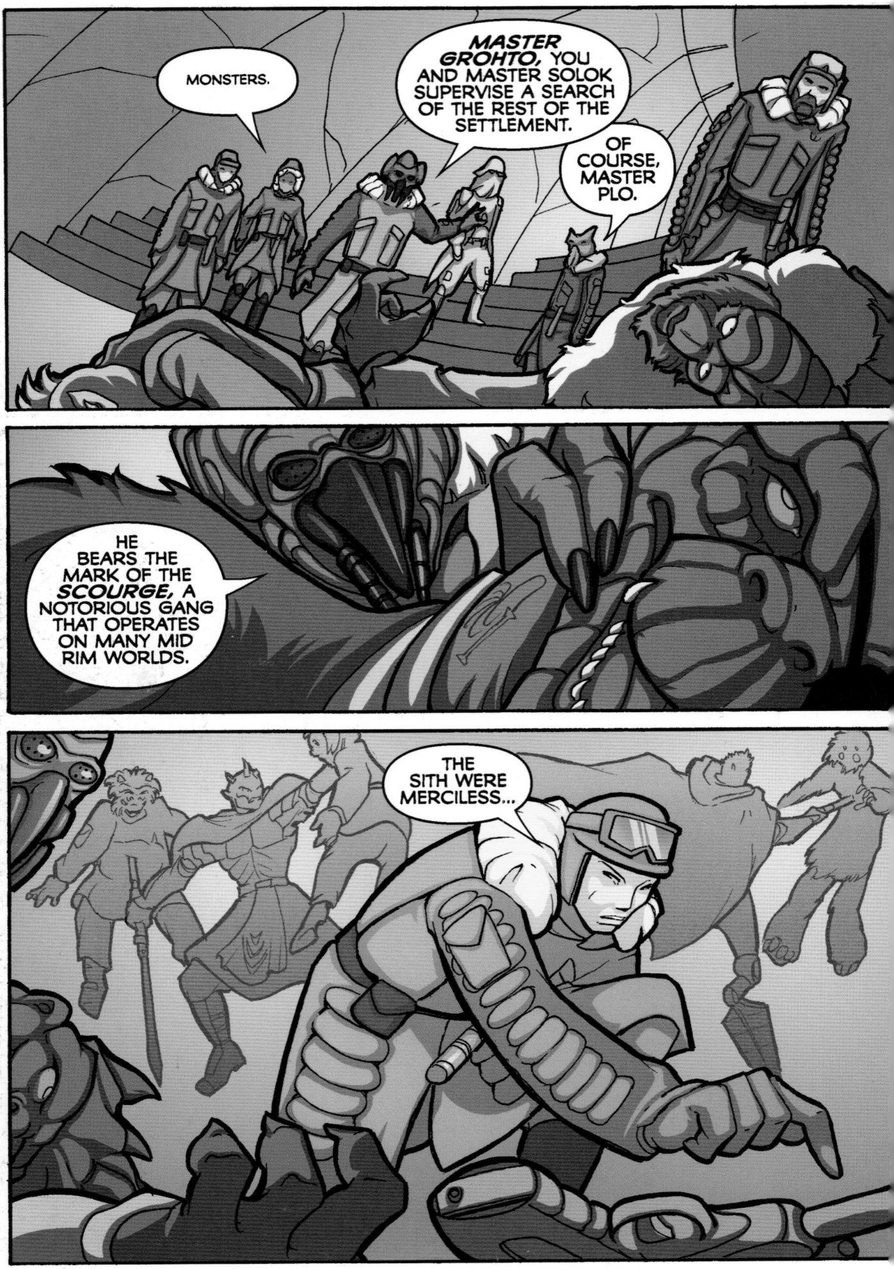
MONSTERS.
MASTER GROHTO, YOU AND MASTER SOLOK SUPERVISE A SEARCH OF THE REST OF THE SETTLEMENT.
OF COURSE, MASTER PLO.
HE BEARS THE MARK OF THE SCOURGE, A NOTORIOUS GANG THAT OPERATES ON MANY MID RIM WORLDS.
THE SITH WERE MERCILESS...

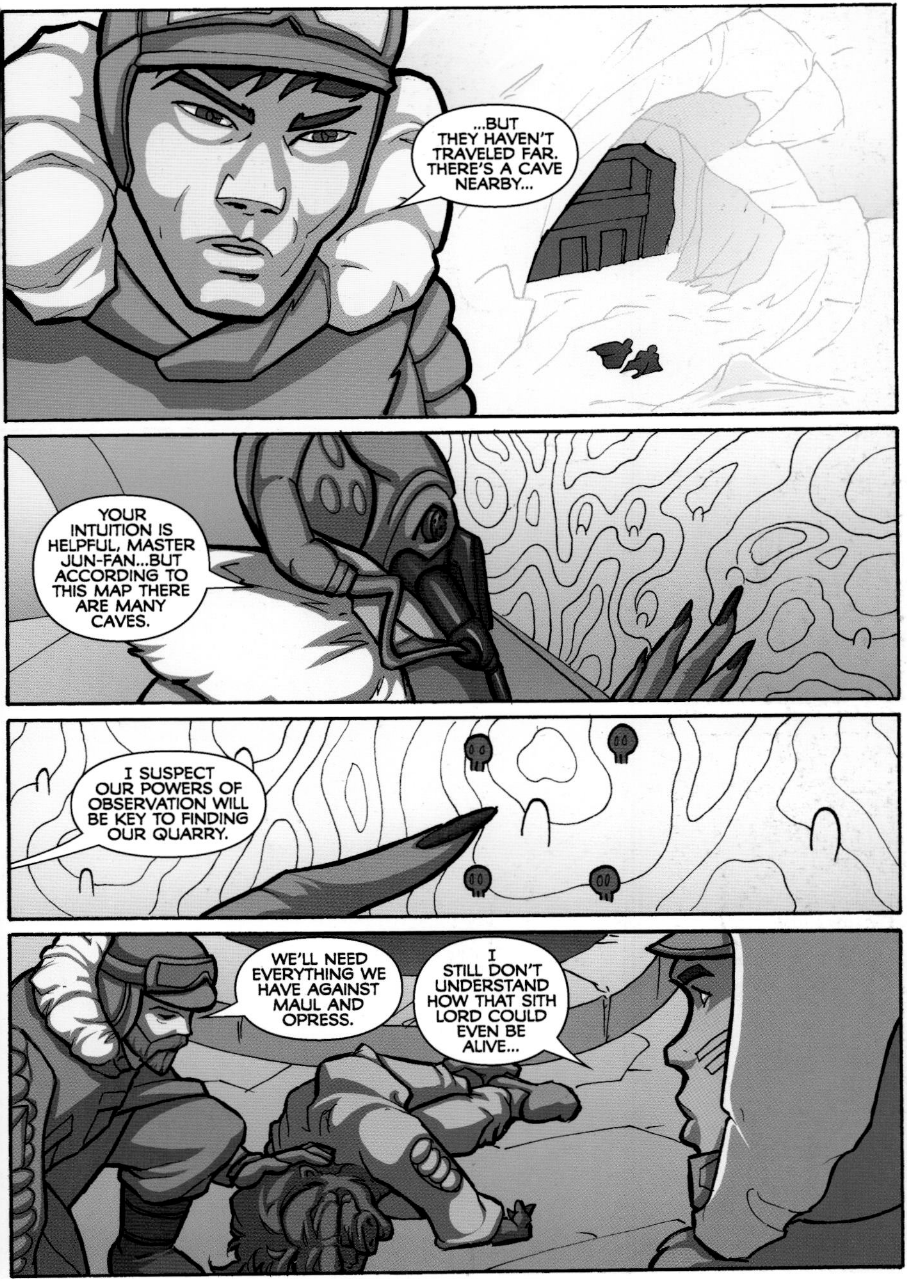
...BUT THEY HAVEN'T TRAVELED FAR. THERE'S A CAVE NEARBY...
YOUR INTUITION IS HELPFUL, MASTER JUN-FAN...BUT ACCORDING TO THIS MAP THERE ARE MANY CAVES.
I SUSPECT OUR POWERS OF OBSERVATION WILL BE KEY TO FINDING OUR QUARRY.
WE'LL NEED EVERYTHING WE HAVE AGAINST MAUL AND OPRESS.
I STILL DON'T UNDERSTAND HOW THAT SITH LORD COULD EVEN BE ALIVE...

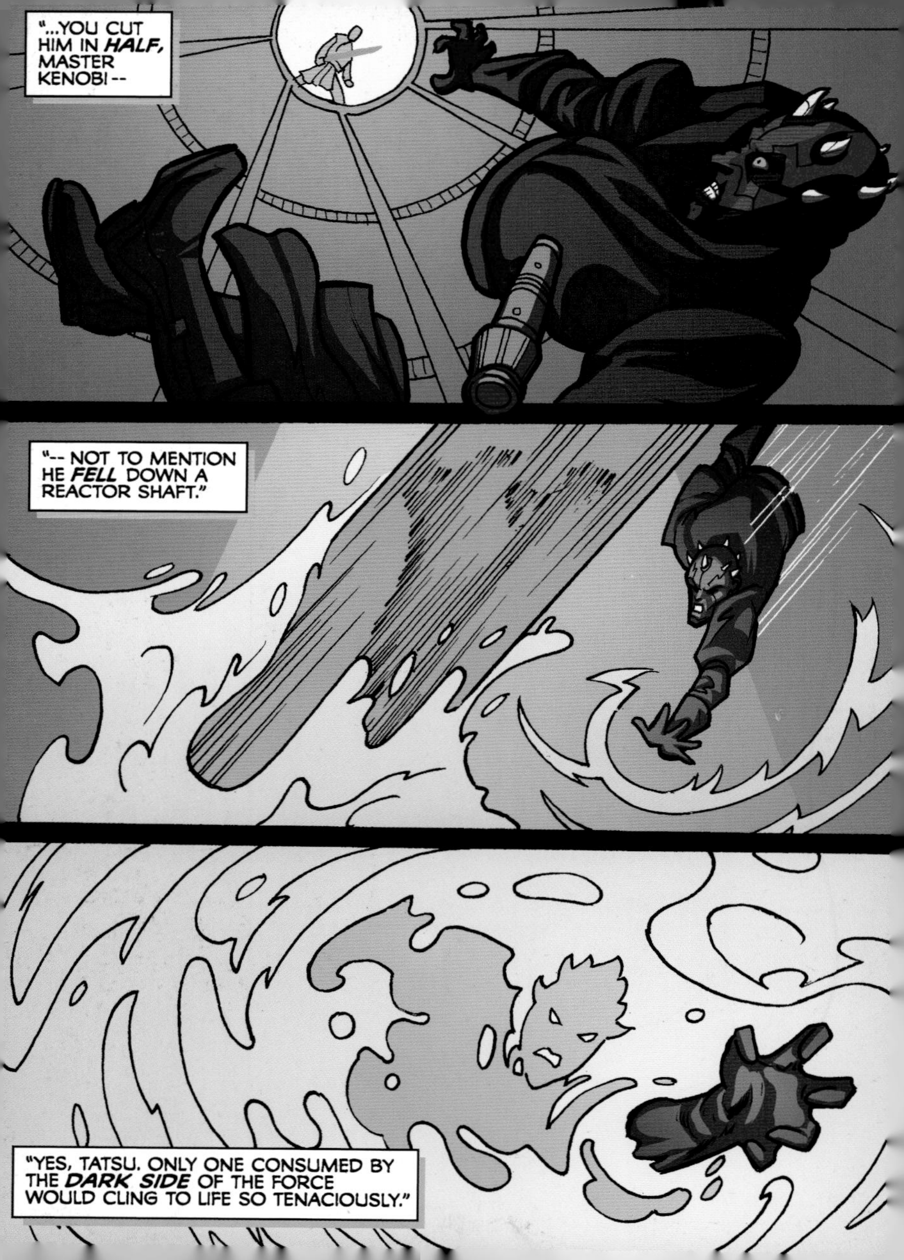
"...YOU CUT HIM IN HALF, MASTER KENOBI --
"-- NOT TO MENTION HE FELL DOWN A REACTOR SHAFT."
"YES, TATSU. ONLY ONE CONSUMED BY THE DARK SIDE OF THE FORCE WOULD CLING TO LIFE SO TENACIOUSLY."

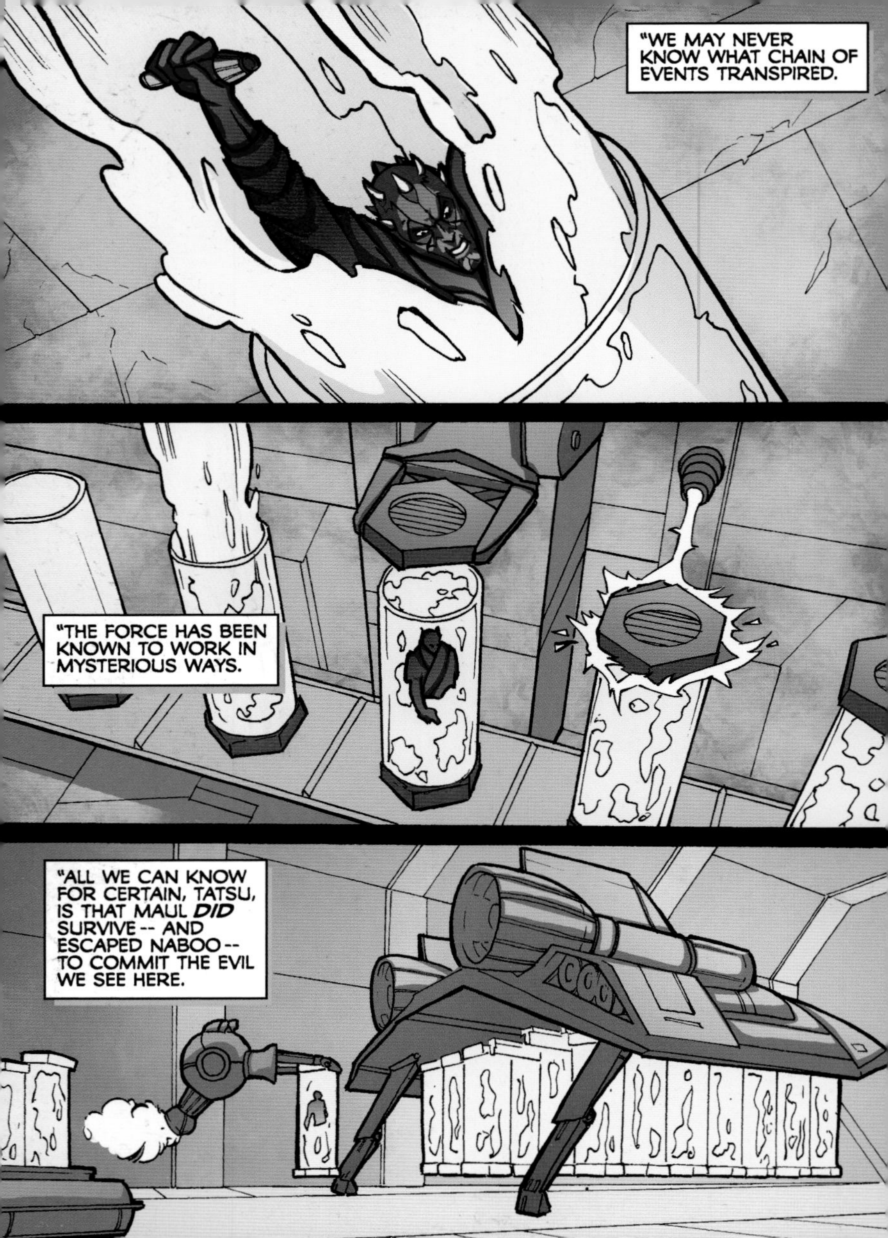
"WE MAY NEVER KNOW WHAT CHAIN OF EVENTS TRANSPIRED.
"THE FORCE HAS BEEN KNOWN TO WORK IN MYSTERIOUS WAYS.
"ALL WE CAN KNOW FOR CERTAIN, TATSU, IS THAT MAUL *DID* SURVIVE -- AND ESCAPED NABOO -- TO COMMIT THE EVIL WE SEE HERE.

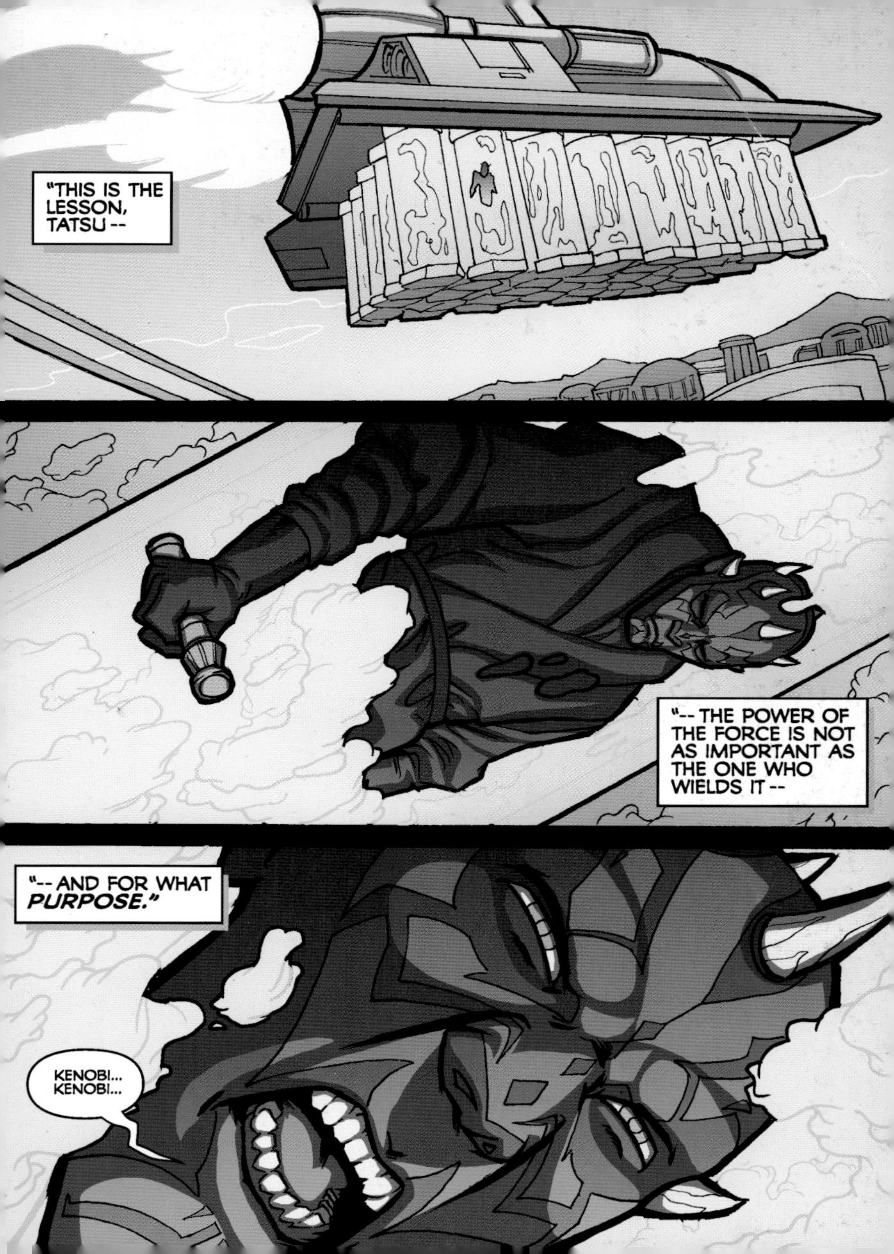
"THIS IS THE LESSON, TATSU --
"-- THE POWER OF THE FORCE IS NOT AS IMPORTANT AS THE ONE WHO WIELDS IT --
"-- AND FOR WHAT PURPOSE."
KENOBI... KENOBI...

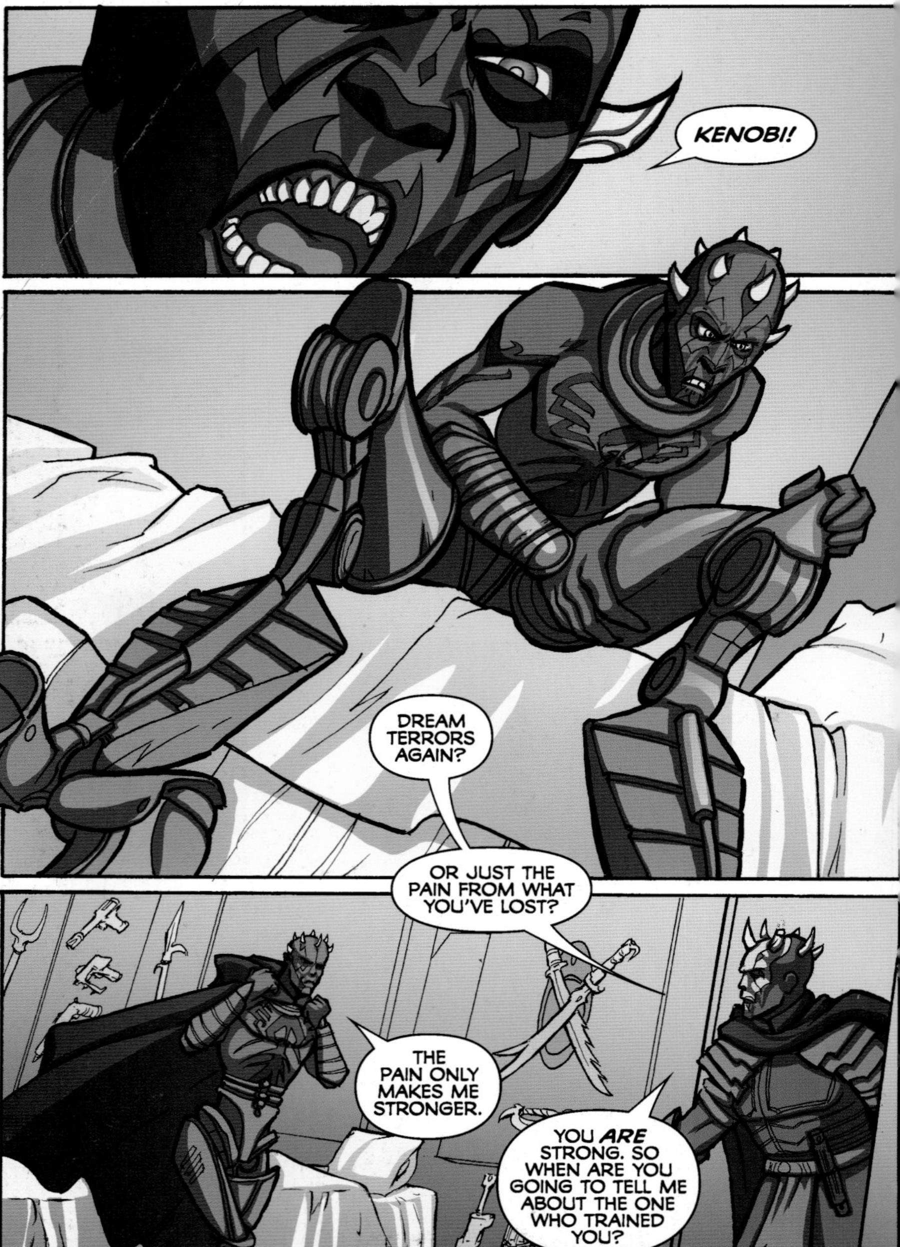
KENOBI!
DREAM TERRORS AGAIN?
OR JUST THE PAIN FROM WHAT YOU'VE LOST?
THE PAIN ONLY MAKES ME STRONGER.
YOU *ARE* STRONG. SO WHEN ARE YOU GOING TO TELL ME ABOUT THE ONE WHO TRAINED YOU?

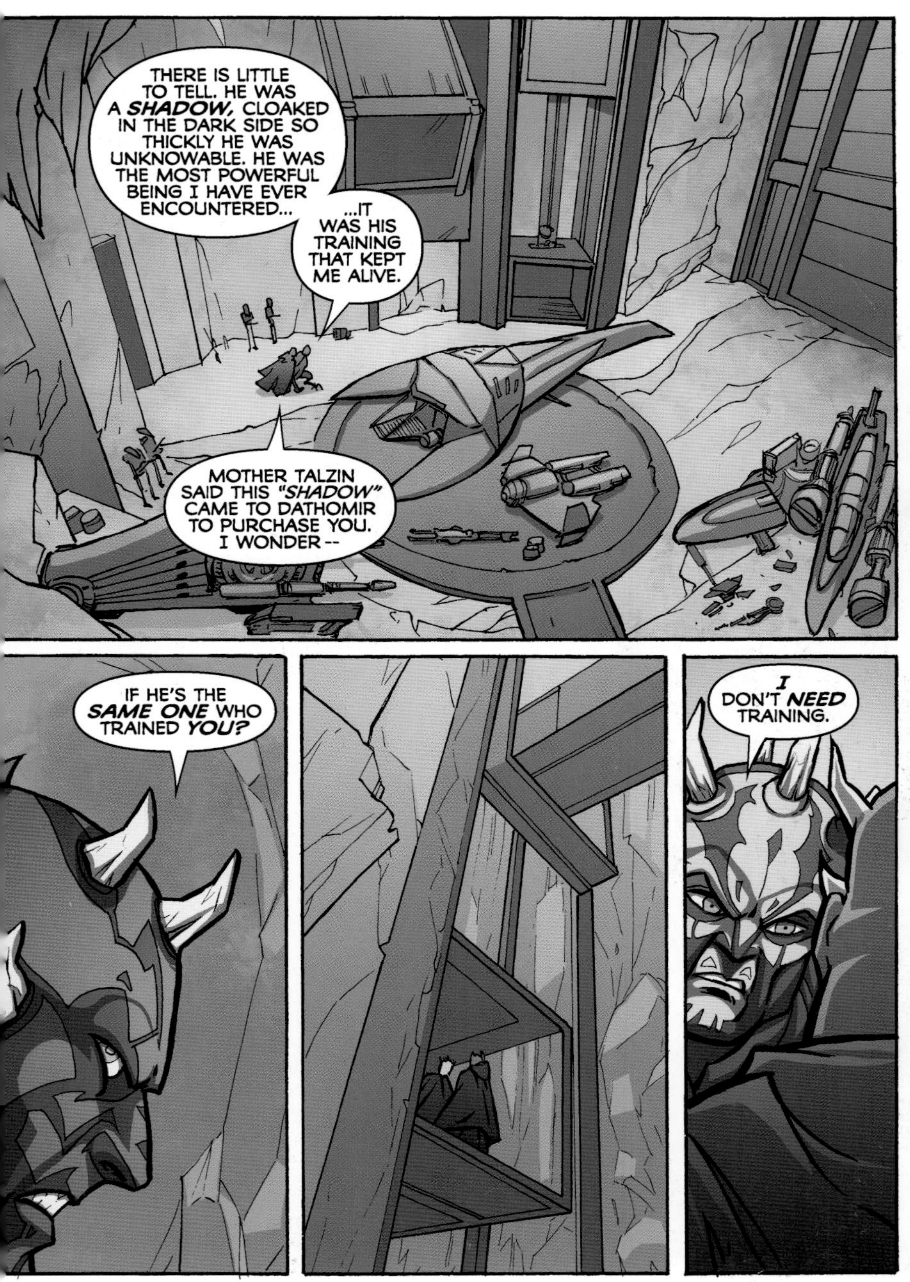
THERE IS LITTLE TO TELL. HE WAS A SHADOW, CLOAKED IN THE DARK SIDE SO THICKLY HE WAS UNKNOWABLE. HE WAS THE MOST POWERFUL BEING I HAVE EVER ENCOUNTERED...
...IT WAS HIS TRAINING THAT KEPT ME ALIVE.
MOTHER TALZIN SAID THIS "SHADOW" CAME TO DATHOMIR TO PURCHASE YOU. I WONDER--
IF HE'S THE SAME ONE WHO TRAINED YOU?
I DON'T NEED TRAINING.

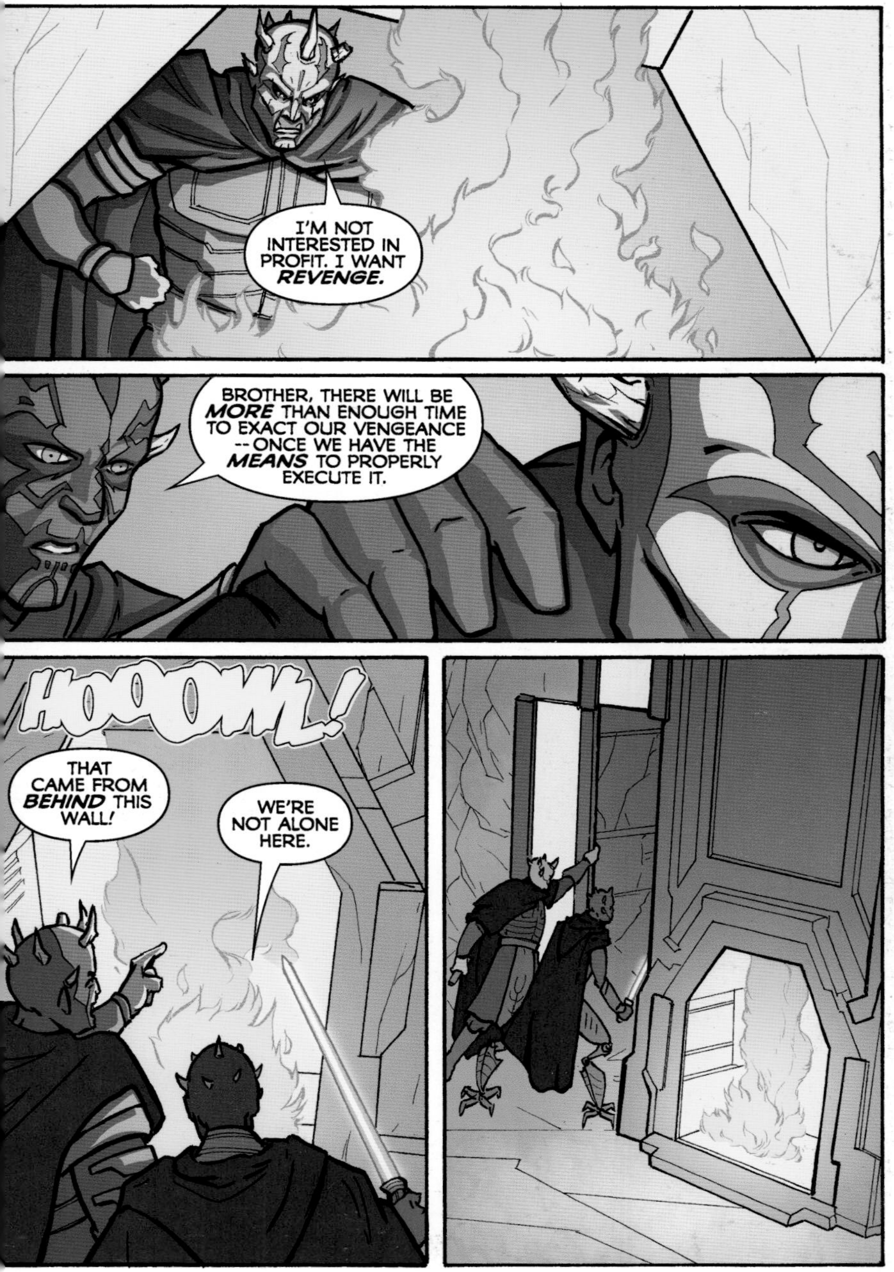

I'M NOT INTERESTED IN PROFIT. I WANT REVENGE.
BROTHER, THERE WILL BE MORE THAN ENOUGH TIME TO EXACT OUR VENGEANCE --ONCE WE HAVE THE MEANS TO PROPERLY EXECUTE IT.
HOOOWL!
THAT CAME FROM BEHIND THIS WALL!
WE'RE NOT ALONE HERE.

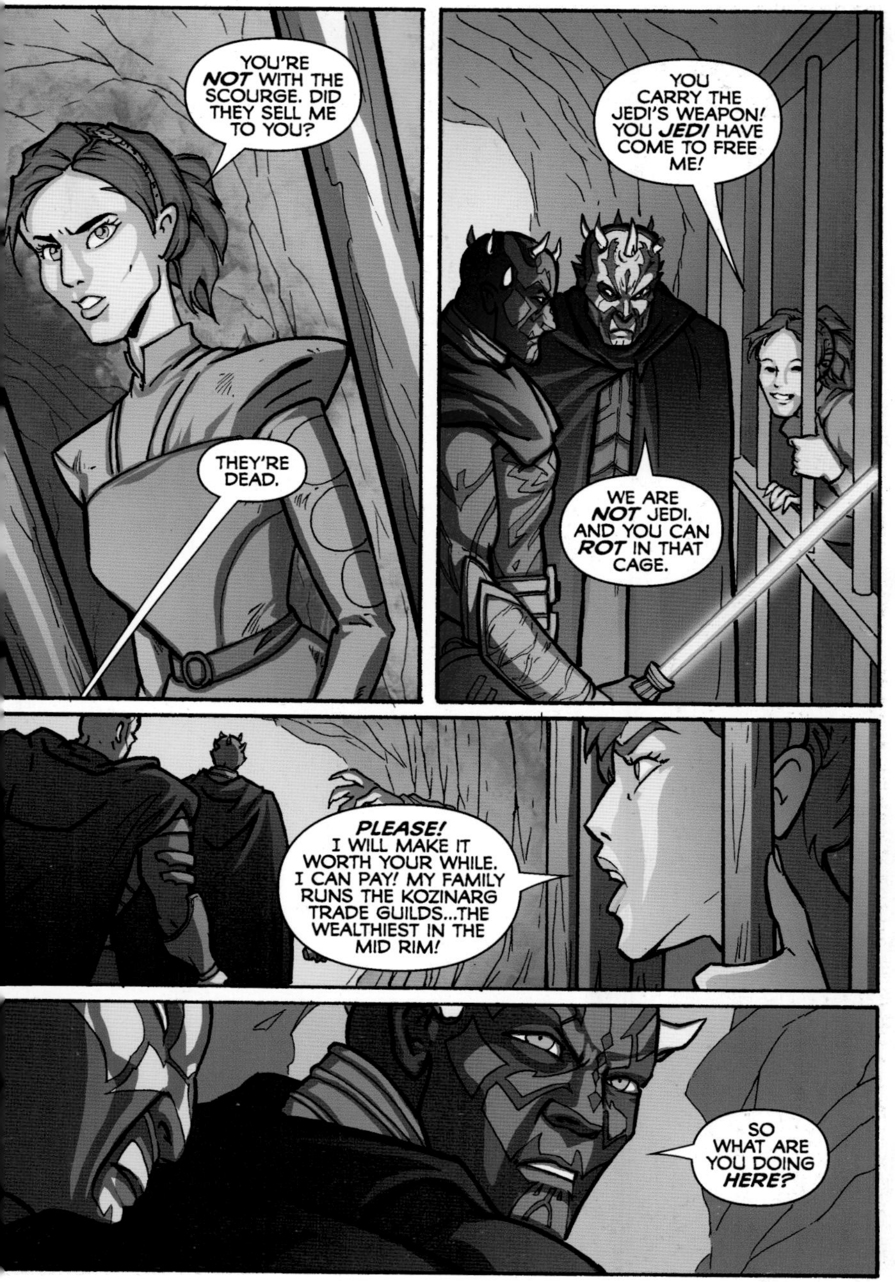
YOU'RE NOT WITH THE SCOURGE. DID THEY SELL ME TO YOU?
THEY'RE DEAD.
YOU CARRY THE JEDI'S WEAPON! YOU JEDI HAVE COME TO FREE ME!
WE ARE NOT JEDI. AND YOU CAN ROT IN THAT CAGE.
PLEASE! I WILL MAKE IT WORTH YOUR WHILE. I CAN PAY! MY FAMILY RUNS THE KOZINARG TRADE GUILDS...THE WEALTHIEST IN THE MID RIM!
SO WHAT ARE YOU DOING HERE?

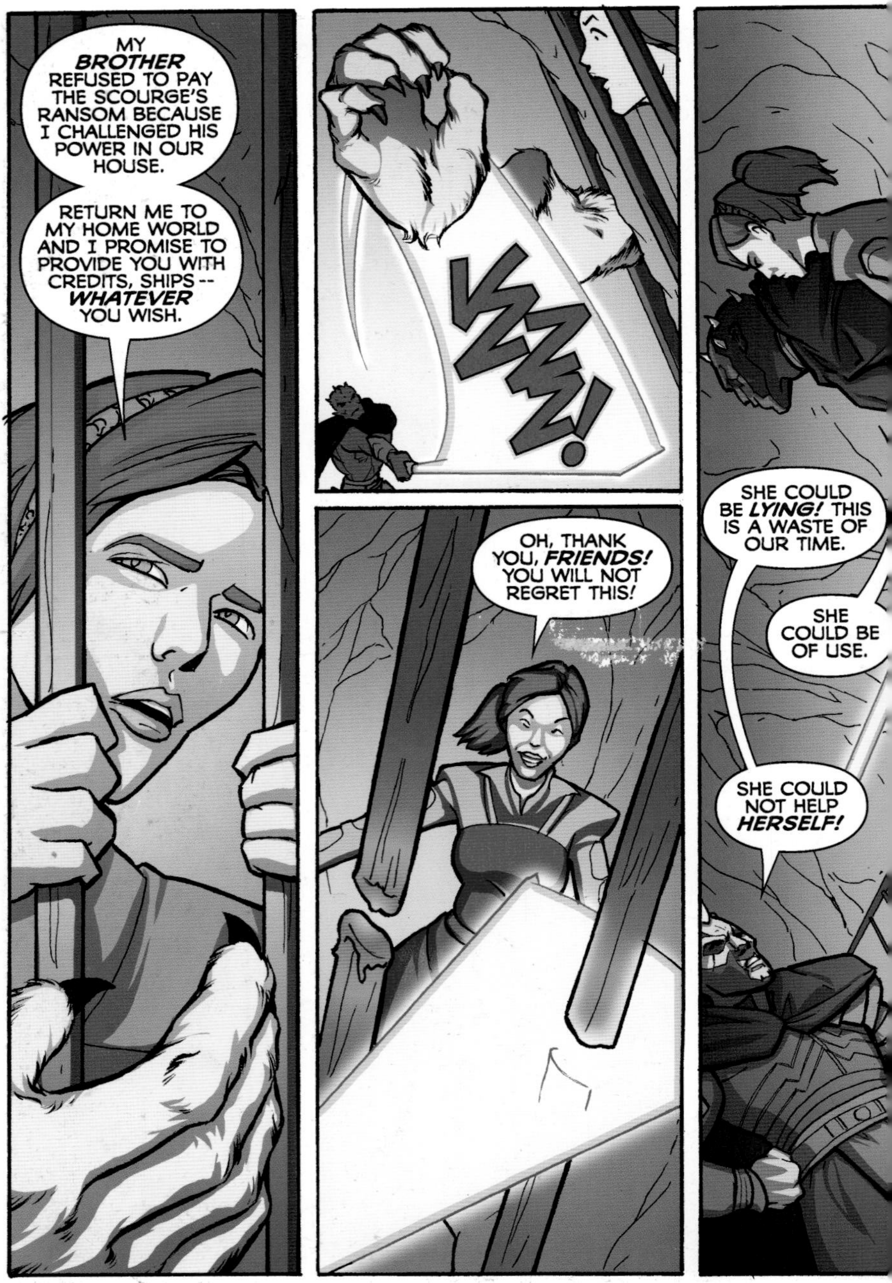

MY **BROTHER** REFUSED TO PAY THE SCOURGE'S RANSOM BECAUSE I CHALLENGED HIS POWER IN OUR HOUSE.
RETURN ME TO MY HOME WORLD AND I PROMISE TO PROVIDE YOU WITH CREDITS, SHIPS -- **WHATEVER** YOU WISH.
VZZZM!
OH, THANK YOU, **FRIENDS!** YOU WILL NOT REGRET THIS!
SHE COULD BE **LYING!** THIS IS A WASTE OF OUR TIME.
SHE COULD BE OF USE.
SHE COULD NOT HELP **HERSELF!**

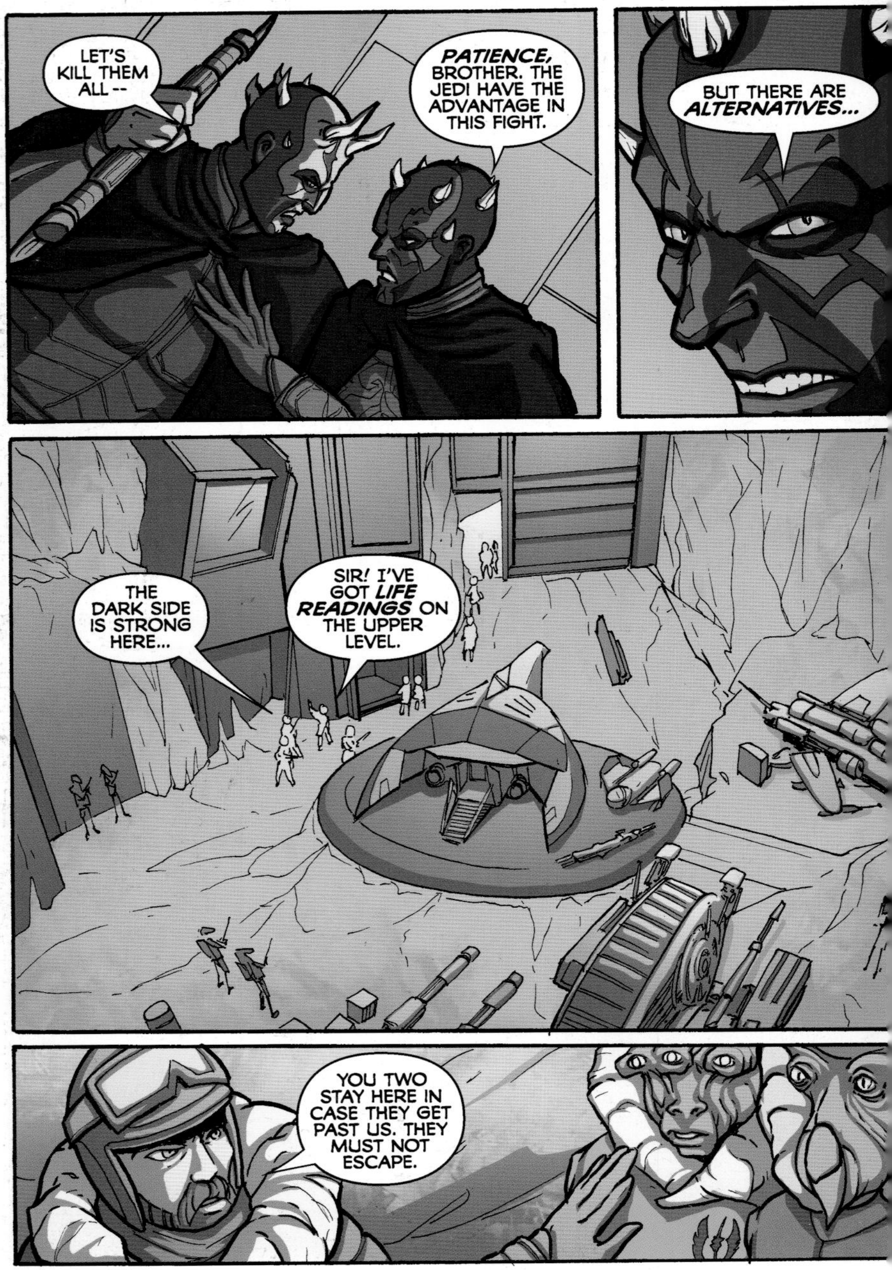
LET'S KILL THEM ALL --
PATIENCE, BROTHER. THE JEDI HAVE THE ADVANTAGE IN THIS FIGHT.
BUT THERE ARE *ALTERNATIVES...*
THE DARK SIDE IS STRONG HERE...
SIR! I'VE GOT *LIFE READINGS* ON THE UPPER LEVEL.
YOU TWO STAY HERE IN CASE THEY GET PAST US. THEY MUST NOT ESCAPE.

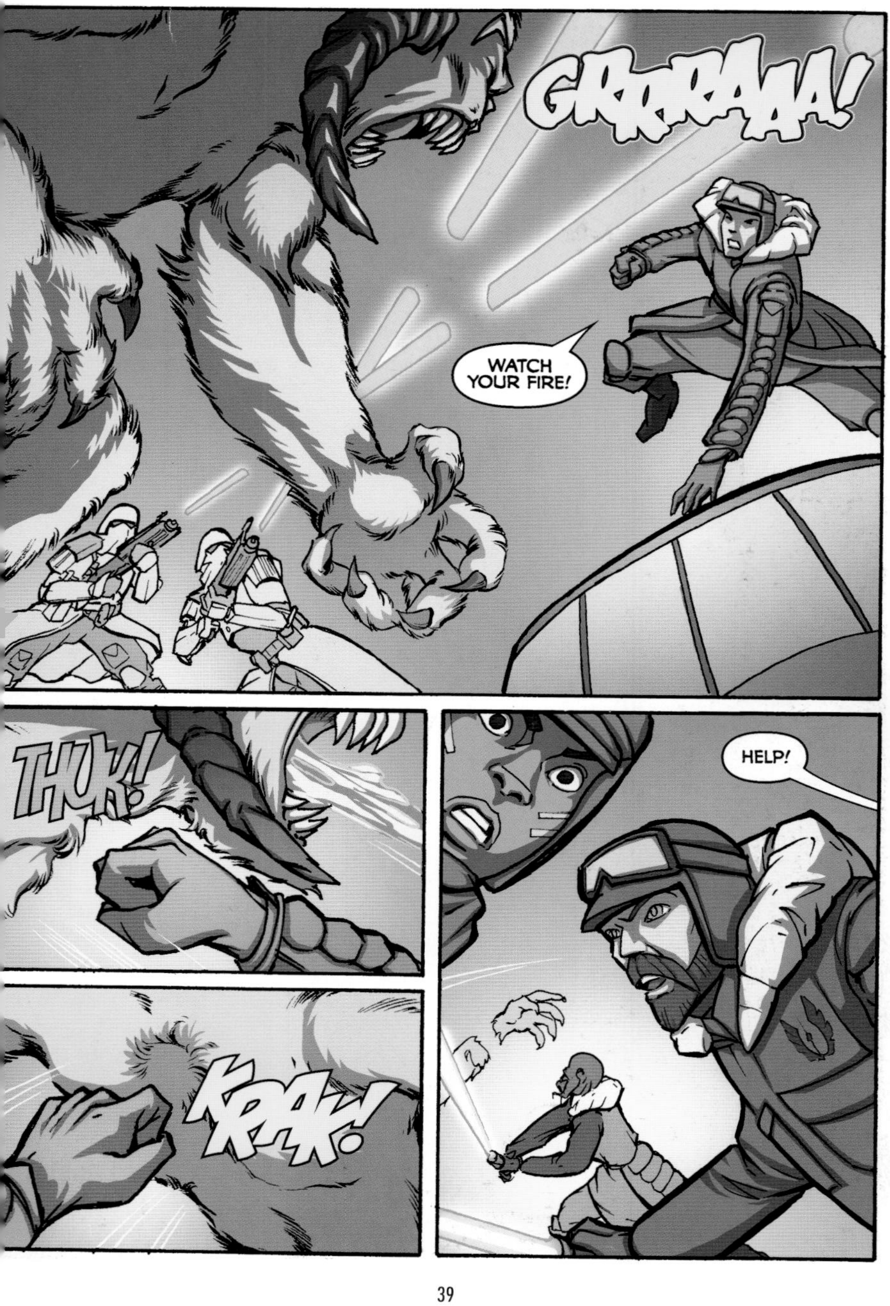
GRRRAAA!
WATCH YOUR FIRE!
THUK!
KRAK!
HELP!

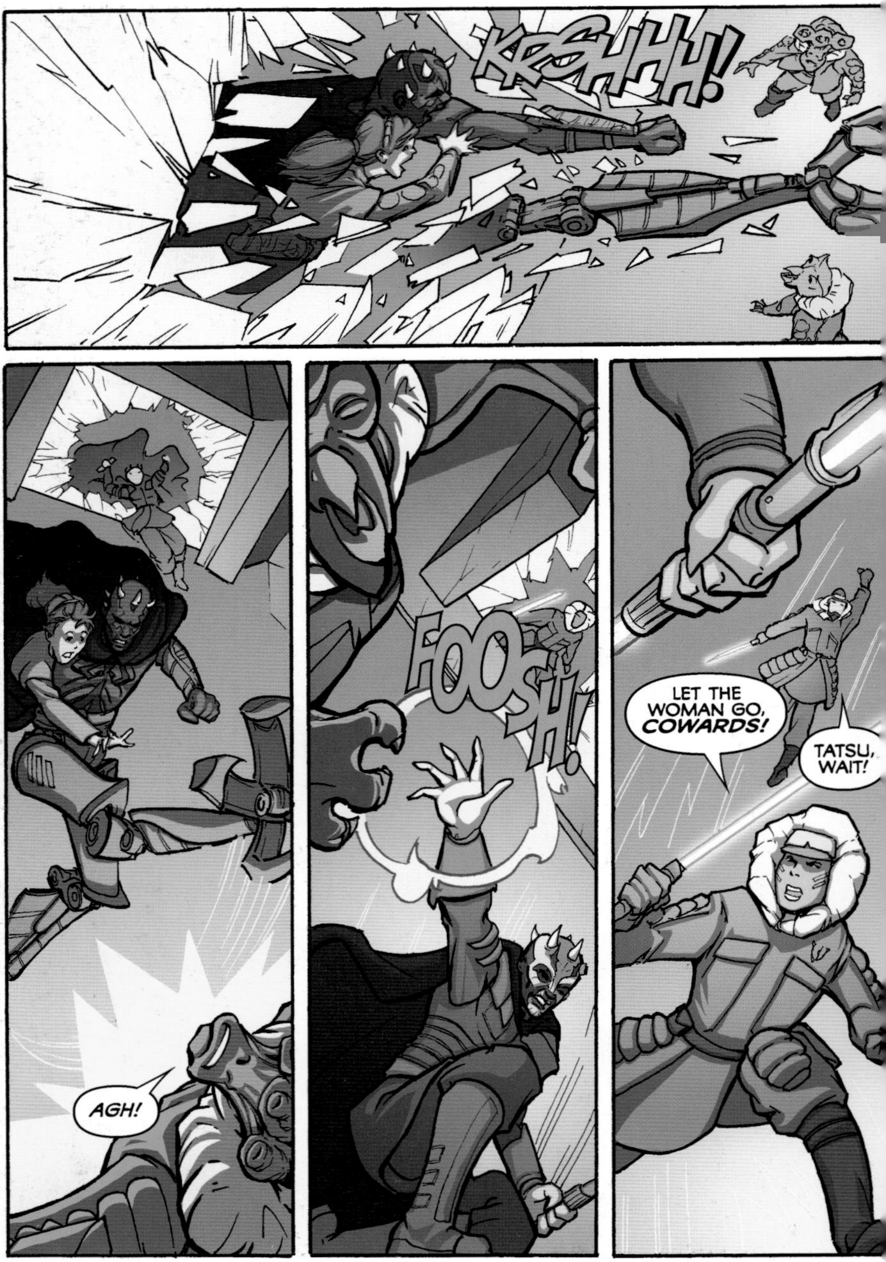
KRSHHH!
AGH!
FOOSH!
LET THE WOMAN GO, ***COWARDS!***
TATSU, WAIT!

SH-NZZZ

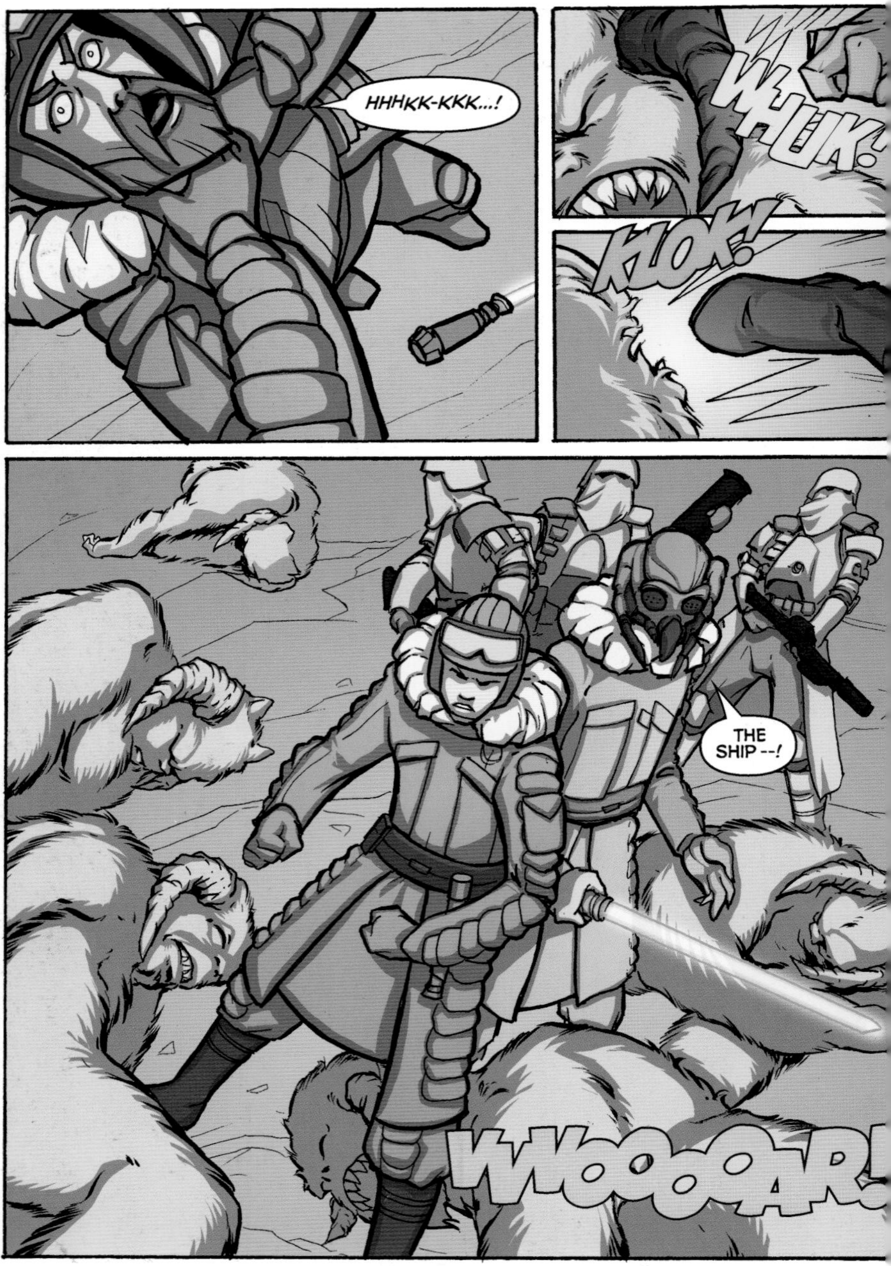
HHHKK-KKK...!
WHUK!
KLOK!
THE SHIP --!
WHOOOOAR!

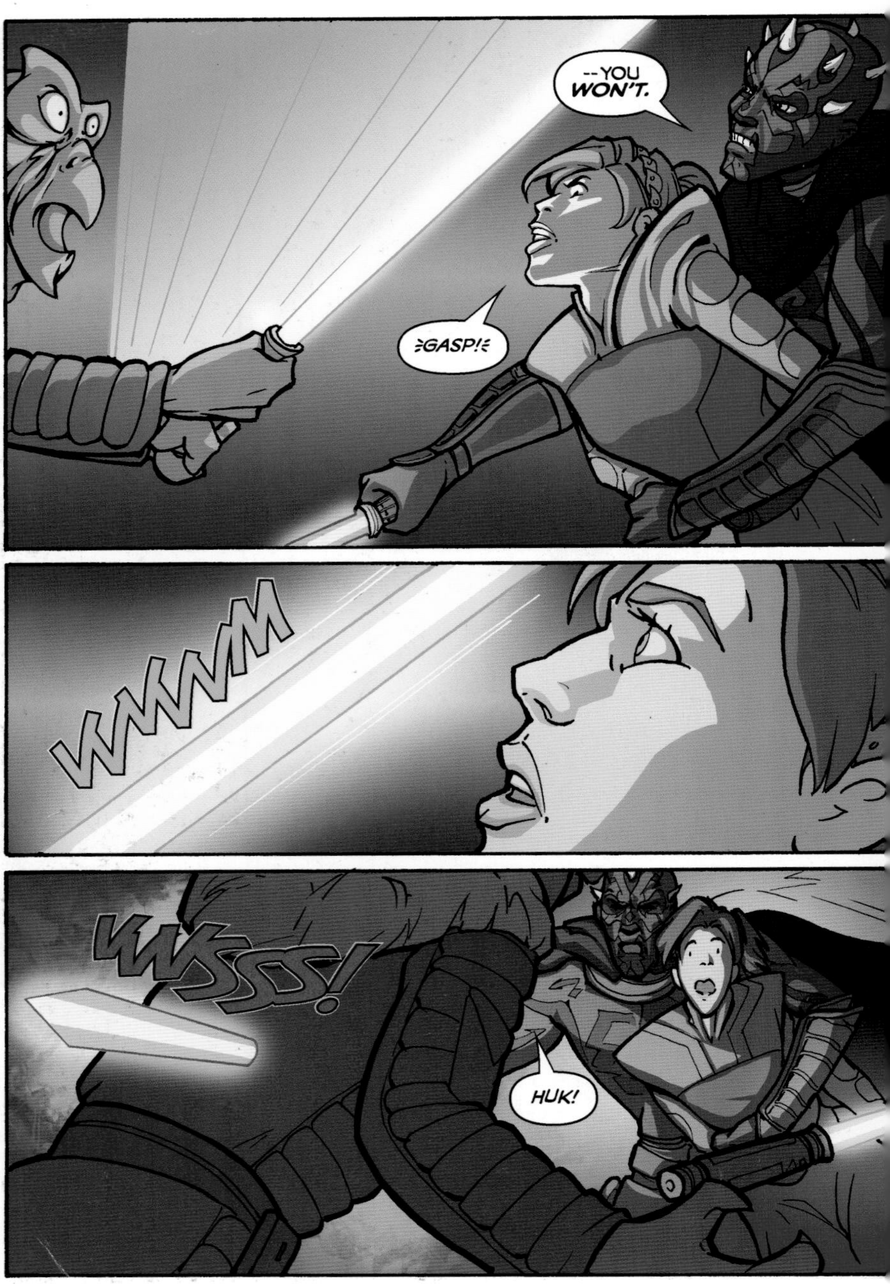
--YOU WON'T.
GASP!
WMMM
KWSSS!
HUK!

46

THE WOMAN DROPPED *THIS*.

I SENSE A CASTLE ON A LAKE. A FAMILY OF SOME IMPORTANCE ON--

I RECOGNIZE THE ARTISTRY OF THIS PIECE. IT IS UNIQUE TO--

YOU HAVE THE EYES OF A *HAWK-BAT*, MASTER PLO. BUT IF YOU'LL ALLOW ME...

--PLEEM'S NEXUS.

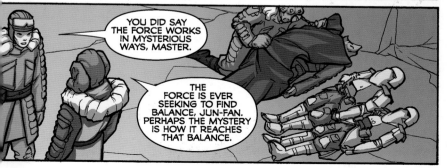

YOU DID SAY THE FORCE WORKS IN MYSTERIOUS WAYS, MASTER.

THE FORCE IS EVER SEEKING TO FIND BALANCE, JUN-FAN. PERHAPS THE MYSTERY IS HOW IT REACHES THAT BALANCE.

47

48

49

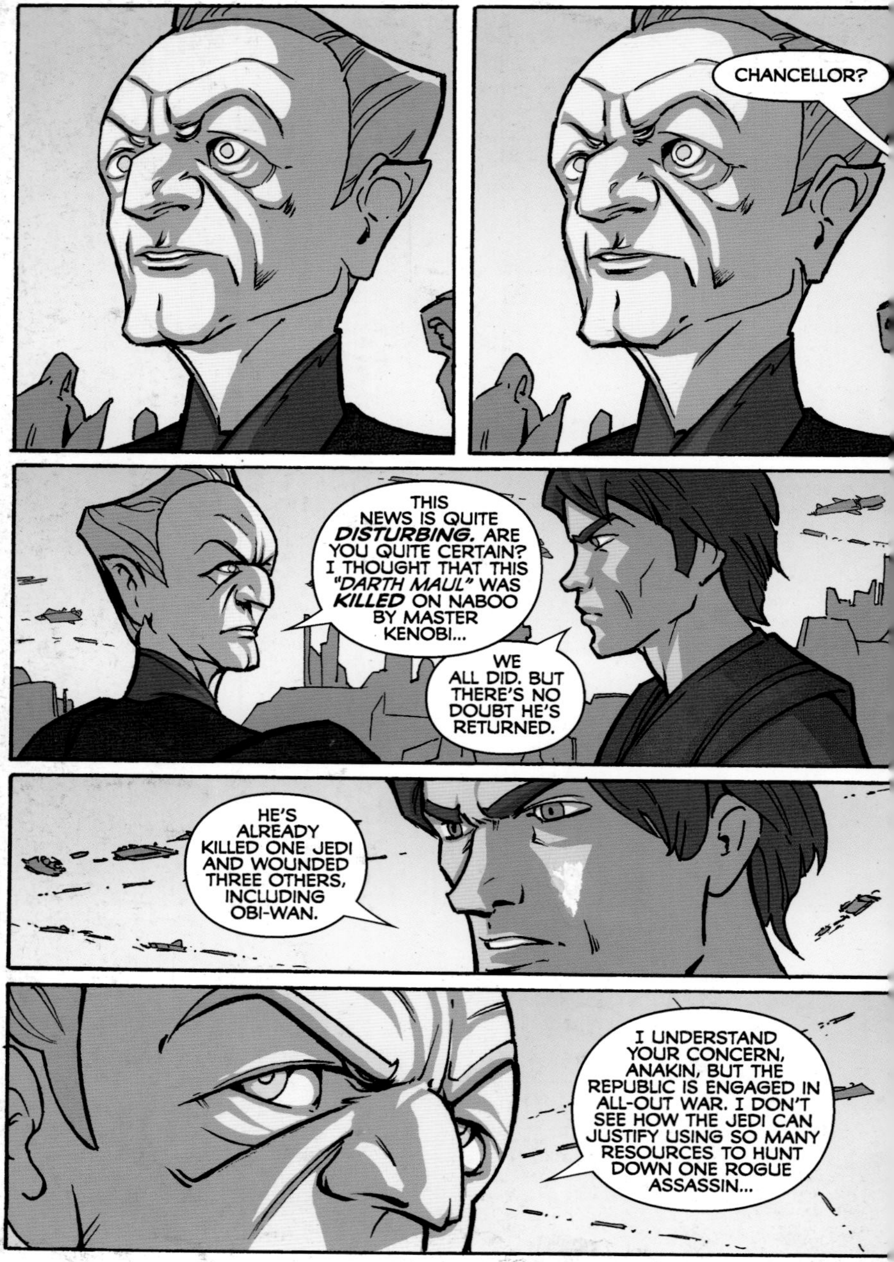
CHANCELLOR?
THIS NEWS IS QUITE *DISTURBING.* ARE YOU QUITE CERTAIN? I THOUGHT THAT THIS *"DARTH MAUL"* WAS *KILLED* ON NABOO BY MASTER KENOBI...
WE ALL DID. BUT THERE'S NO DOUBT HE'S RETURNED.
HE'S ALREADY KILLED ONE JEDI AND WOUNDED THREE OTHERS, INCLUDING OBI-WAN.
I UNDERSTAND YOUR CONCERN, ANAKIN, BUT THE REPUBLIC IS ENGAGED IN ALL-OUT WAR. I DON'T SEE HOW THE JEDI CAN JUSTIFY USING SO MANY RESOURCES TO HUNT DOWN ONE ROGUE ASSASSIN...

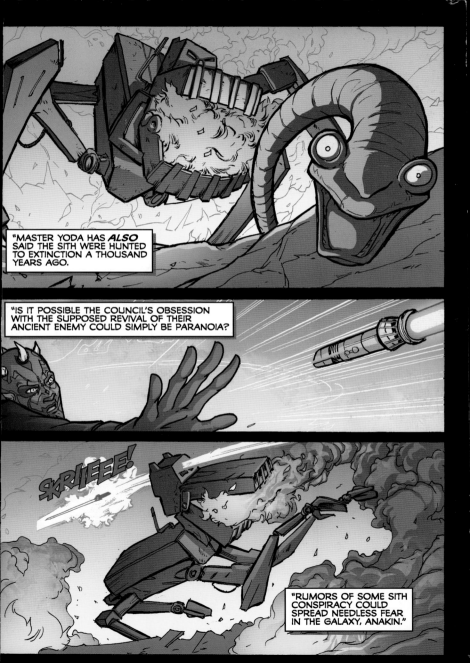

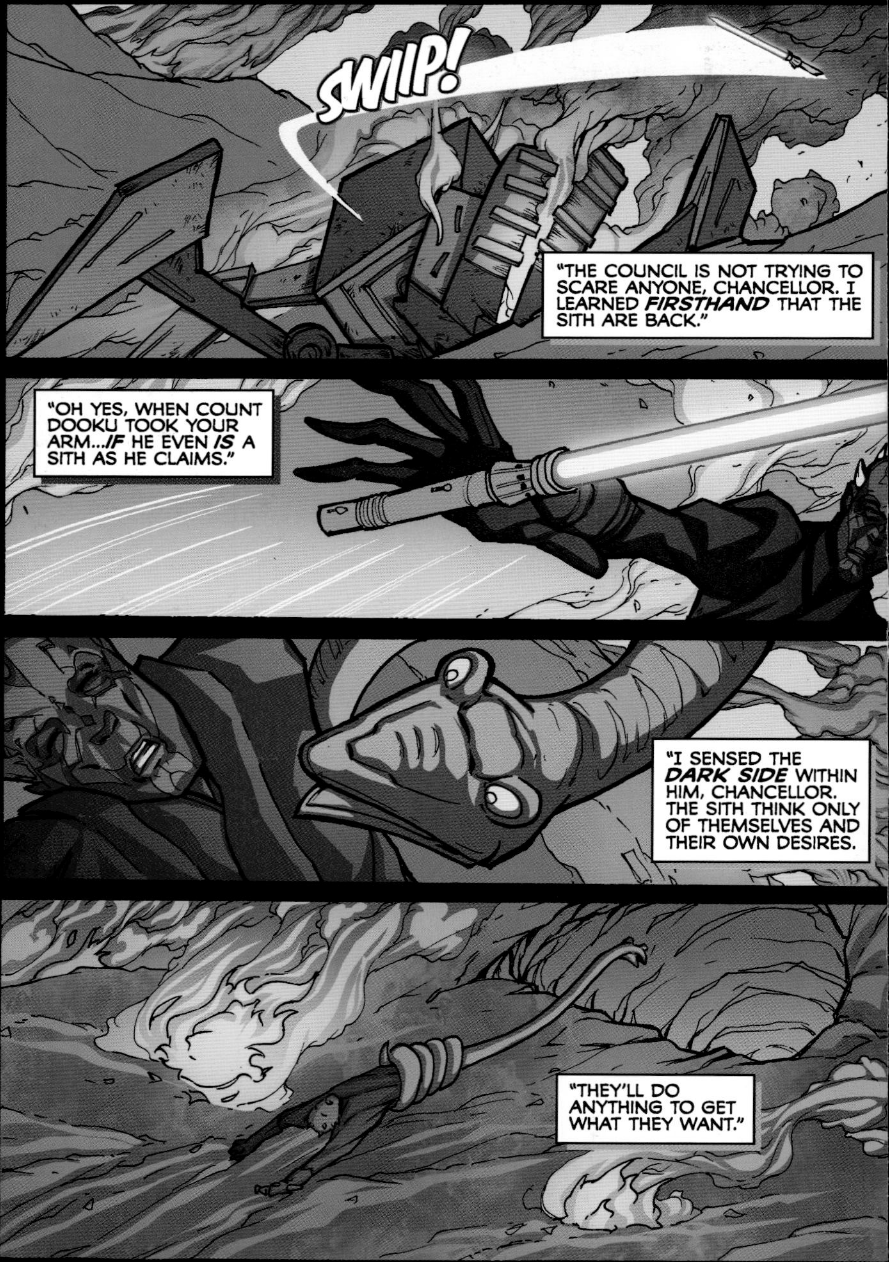
SWIIP!
"THE COUNCIL IS NOT TRYING TO SCARE ANYONE, CHANCELLOR. I LEARNED FIRSTHAND THAT THE SITH ARE BACK."
"OH YES, WHEN COUNT DOOKU TOOK YOUR ARM...IF HE EVEN IS A SITH AS HE CLAIMS."
"I SENSED THE DARK SIDE WITHIN HIM, CHANCELLOR. THE SITH THINK ONLY OF THEMSELVES AND THEIR OWN DESIRES.
"THEY'LL DO ANYTHING TO GET WHAT THEY WANT."

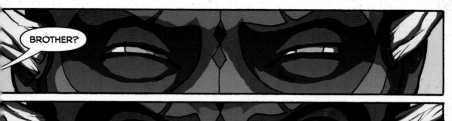

BROTHER?

BROTHER?

WE'VE ARRIVED--

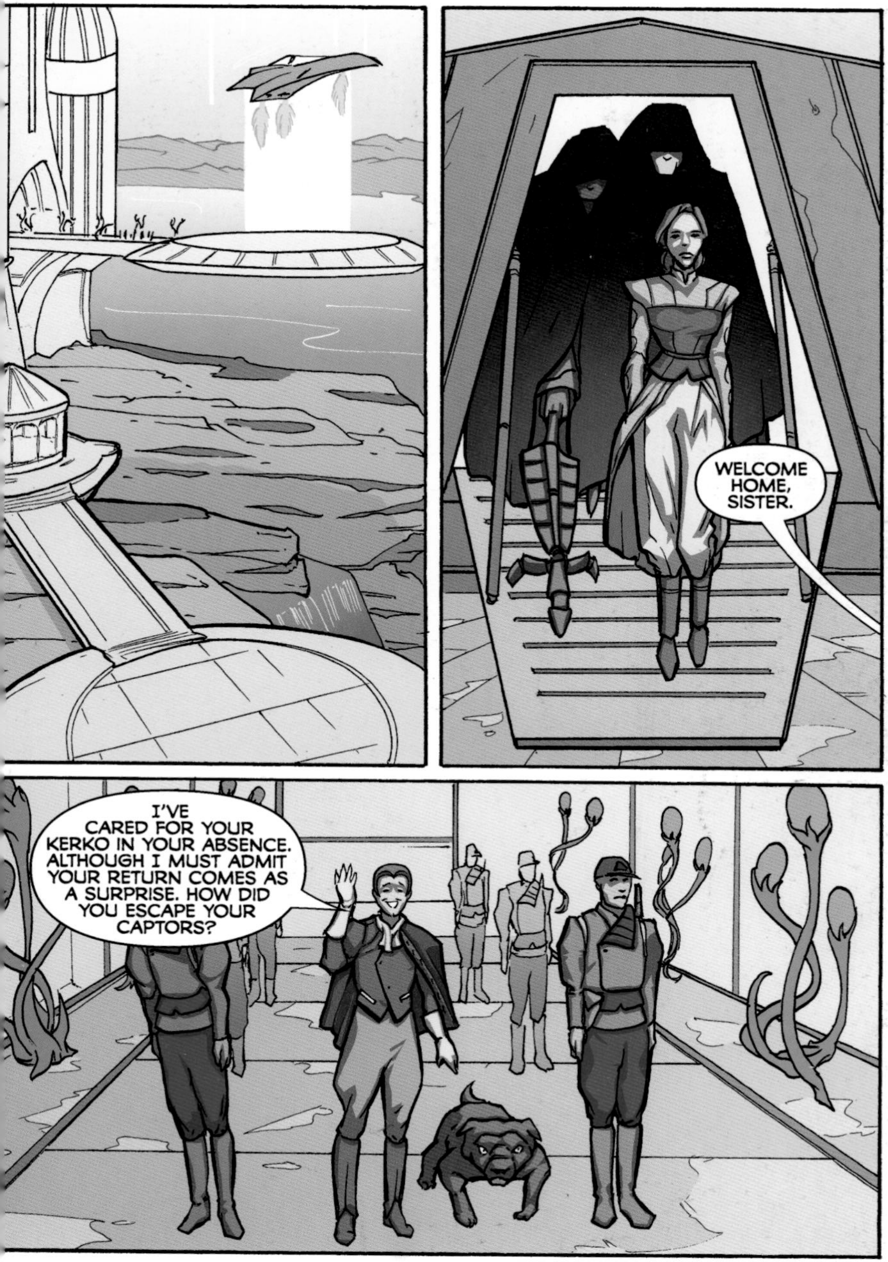
WELCOME HOME, SISTER.
I'VE CARED FOR YOUR KERKO IN YOUR ABSENCE. ALTHOUGH I MUST ADMIT YOUR RETURN COMES AS A SURPRISE. HOW DID YOU ESCAPE YOUR CAPTORS?

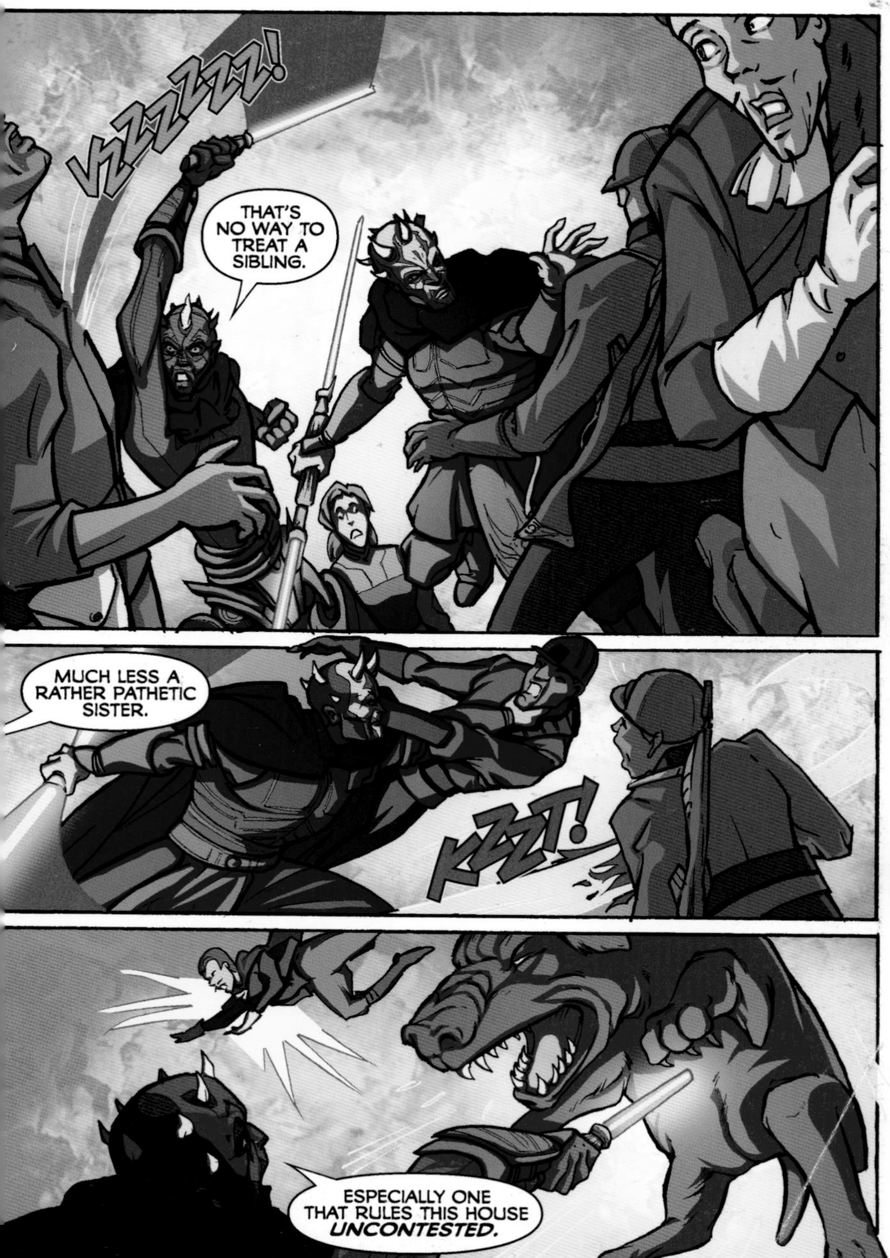
VZZZZZZZ!
THAT'S NO WAY TO TREAT A SIBLING.
MUCH LESS A RATHER PATHETIC SISTER.
KZZT!
ESPECIALLY ONE THAT RULES THIS HOUSE *UNCONTESTED.*

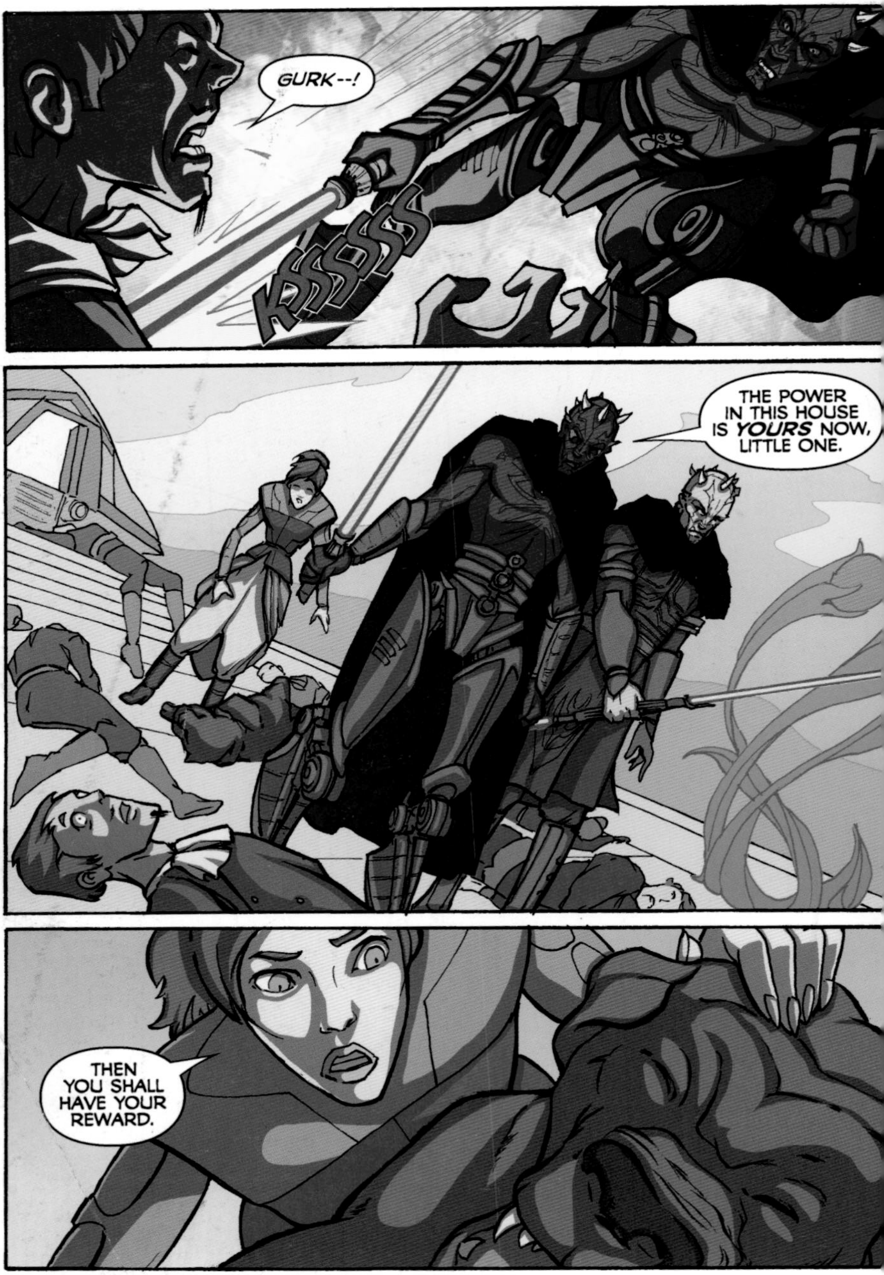
GURK--!
KRSSSSS
THE POWER IN THIS HOUSE IS *YOURS* NOW, LITTLE ONE.
THEN YOU SHALL HAVE YOUR REWARD.

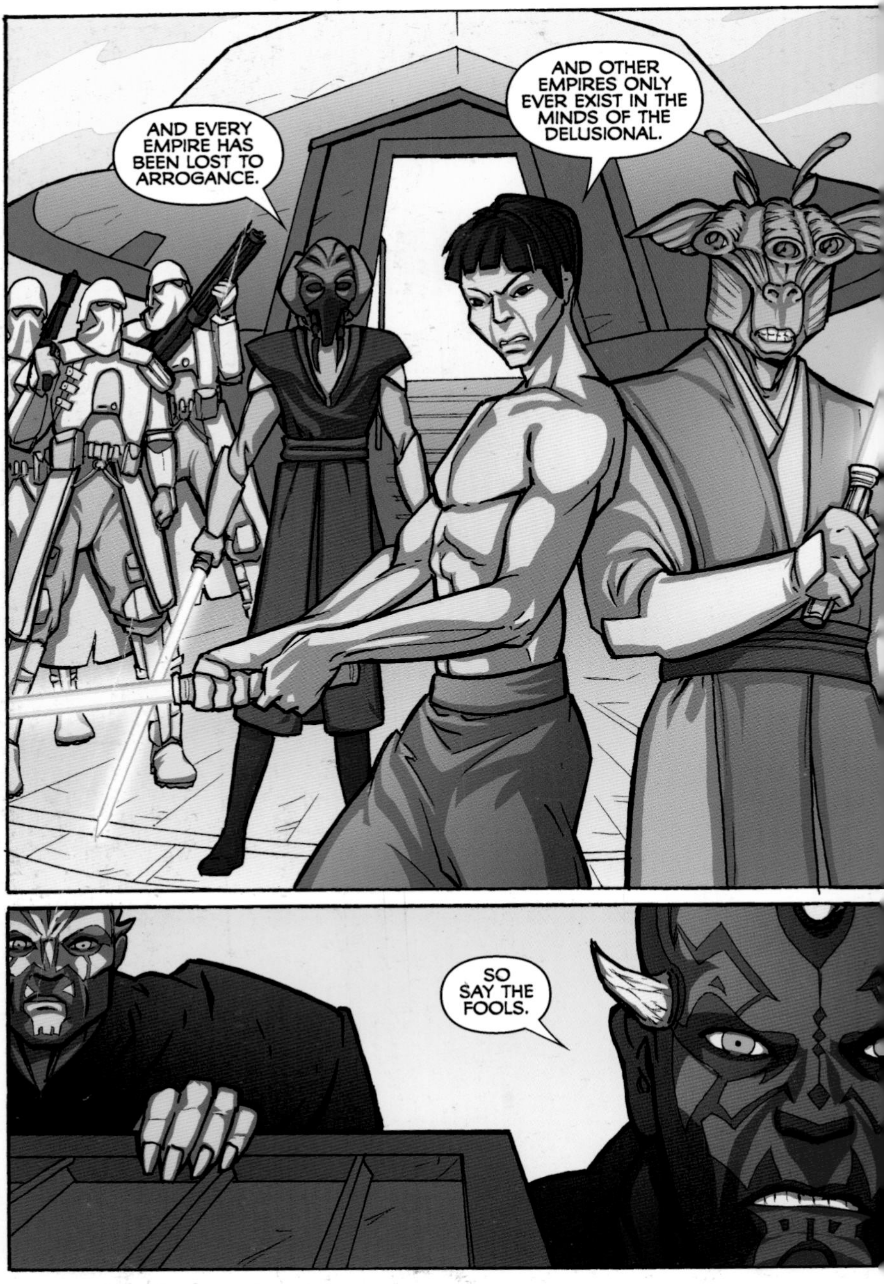
AND EVERY EMPIRE HAS BEEN LOST TO ARROGANCE.
AND OTHER EMPIRES ONLY EVER EXIST IN THE MINDS OF THE DELUSIONAL.
SO SAY THE FOOLS.

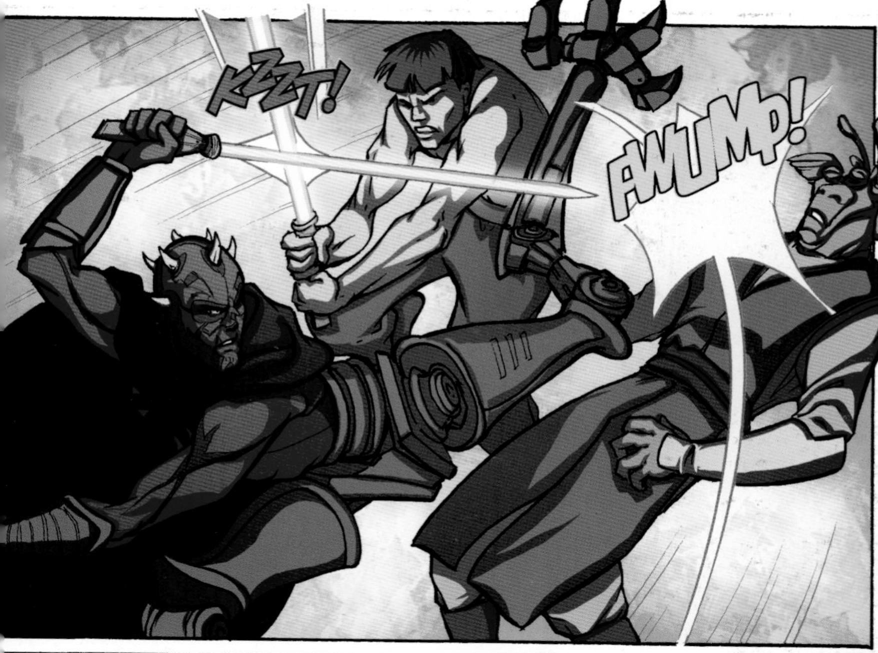
KZZZT!
FWUMP!

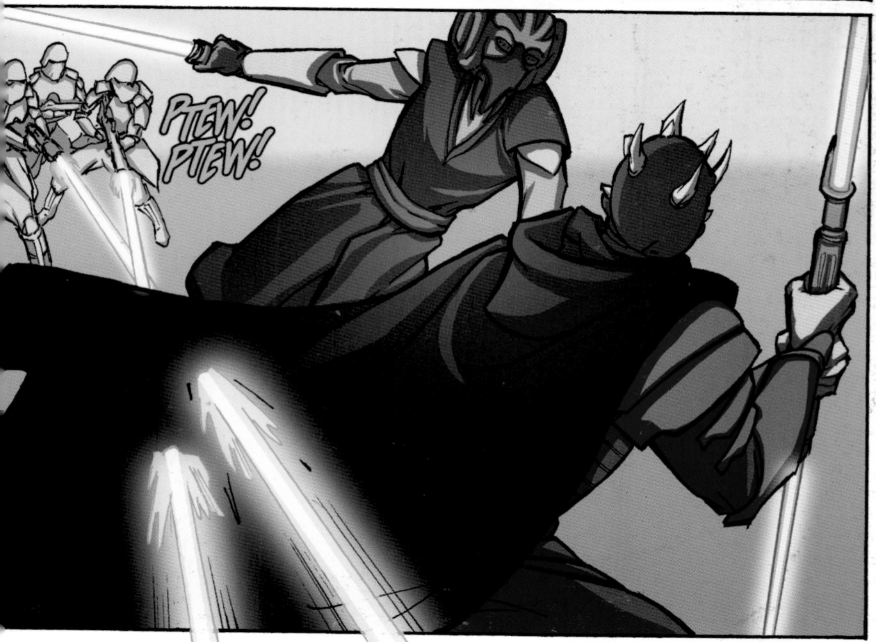
PTEW! PTEW!

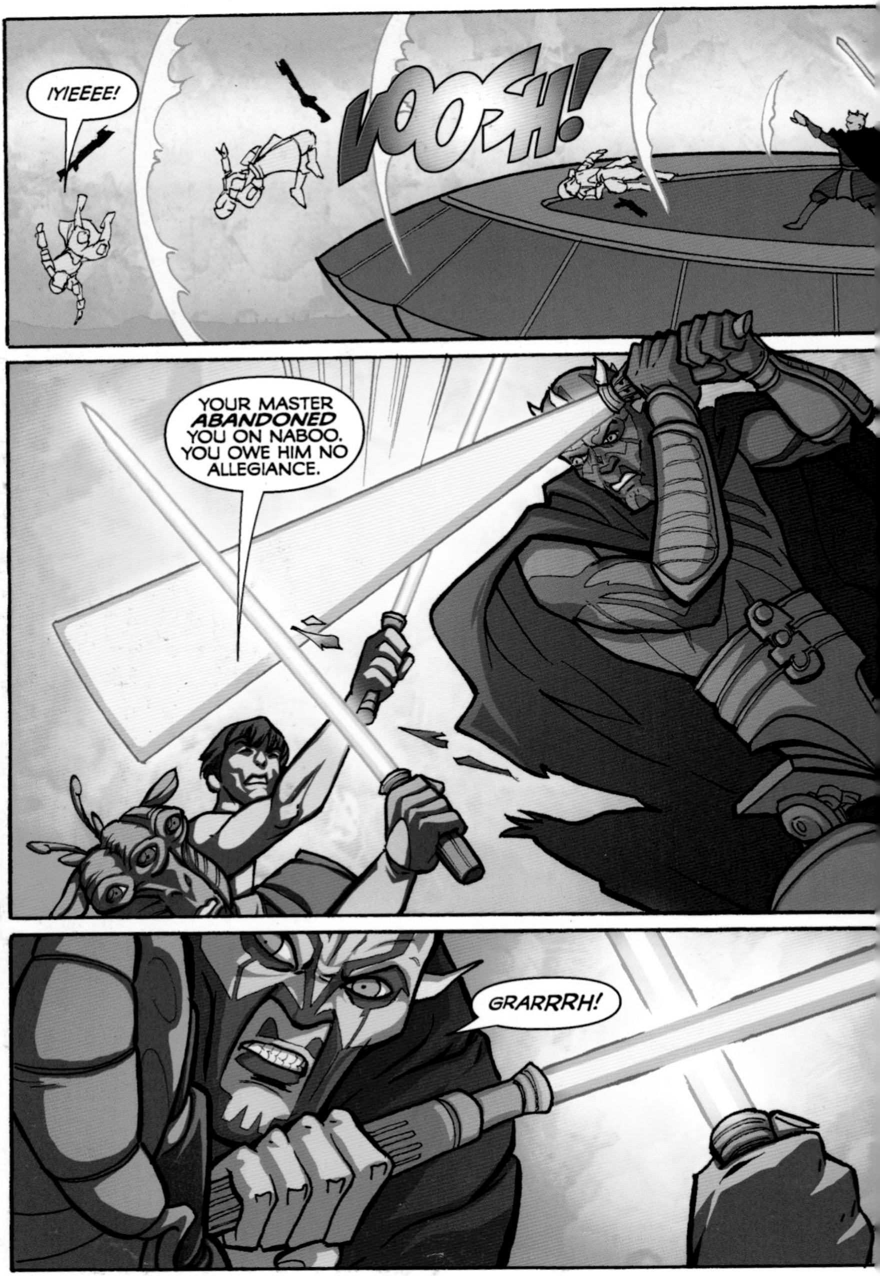
IYIEEEE!
VOOSH!
YOUR MASTER ABANDONED YOU ON NABOO. YOU OWE HIM NO ALLEGIANCE.
GRARRRH!

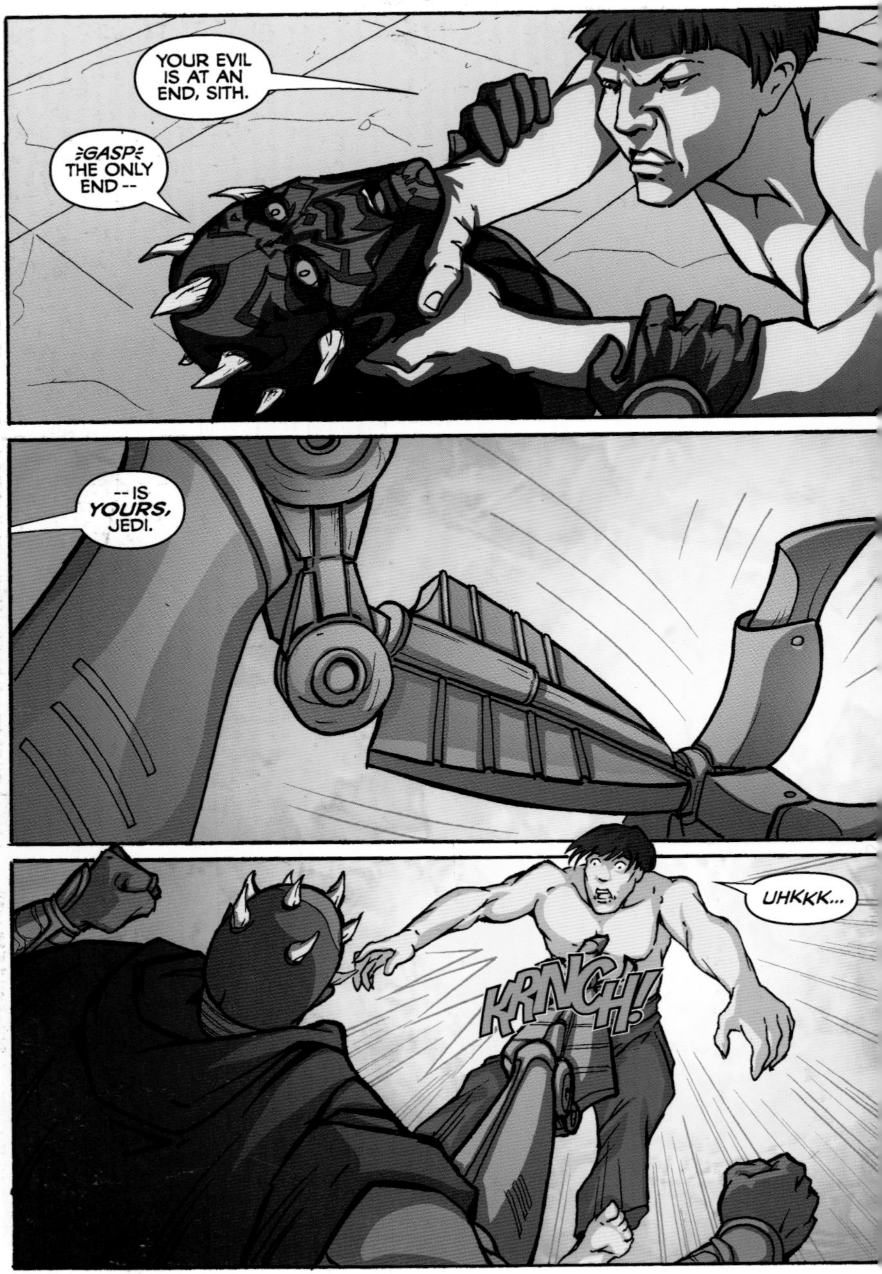
YOUR EVIL IS AT AN END, SITH.
GASP THE ONLY END --
-- IS YOURS, JEDI.
UHKKK...
KRNCH!

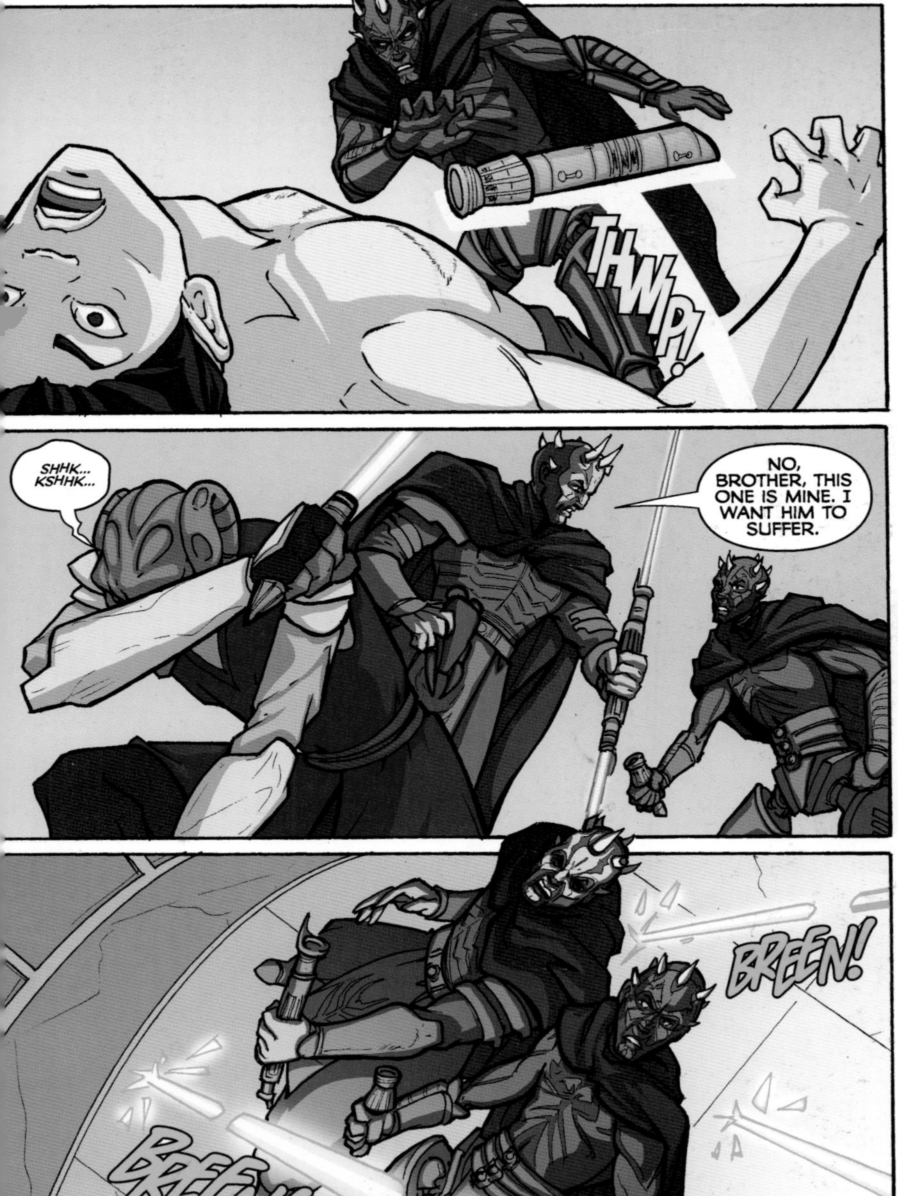
THWIP!
SHHK... KSHHK...
NO, BROTHER, THIS ONE IS MINE. I WANT HIM TO SUFFER.
BREEN!
BREEN!

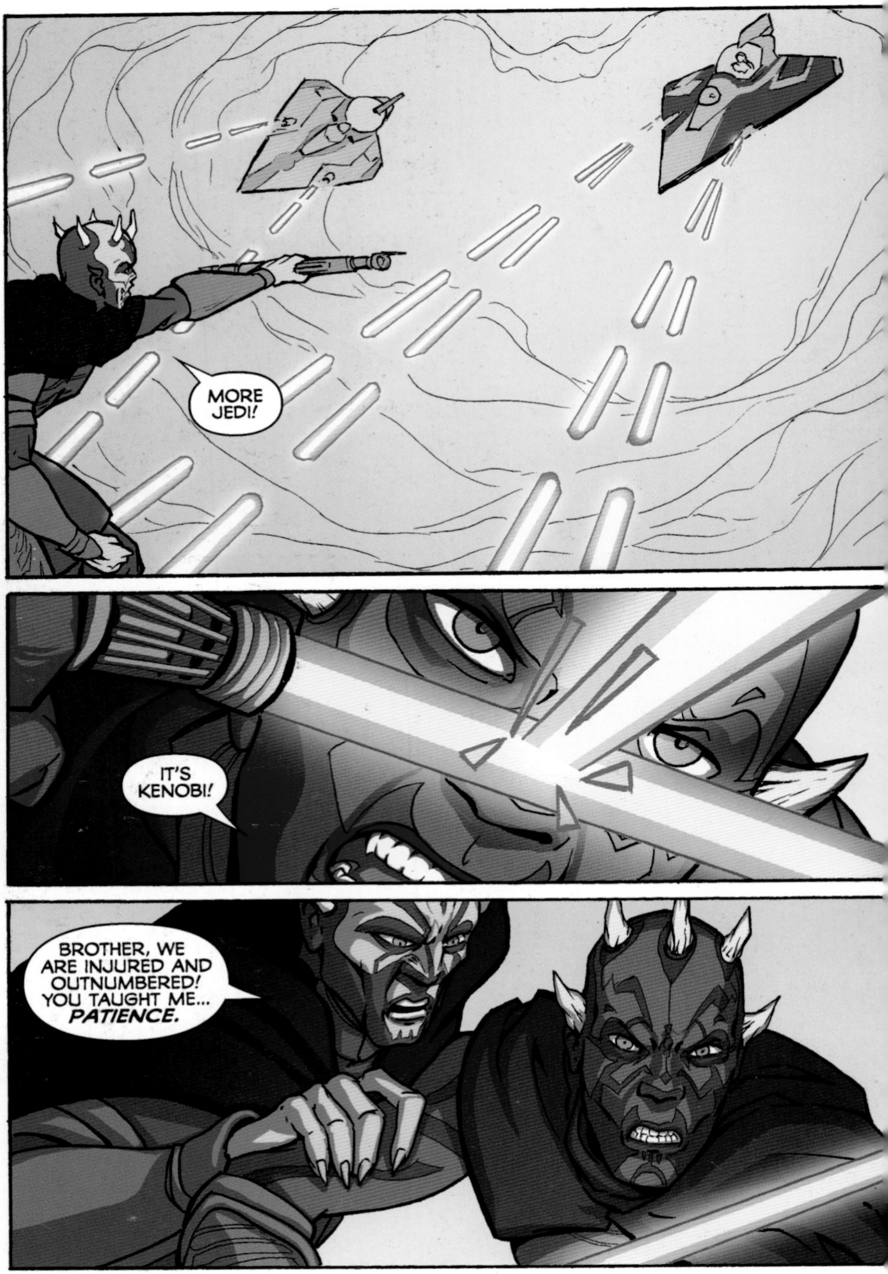
MORE JEDI!
IT'S KENOBI!
BROTHER, WE ARE INJURED AND OUTNUMBERED! YOU TAUGHT ME... *PATIENCE.*

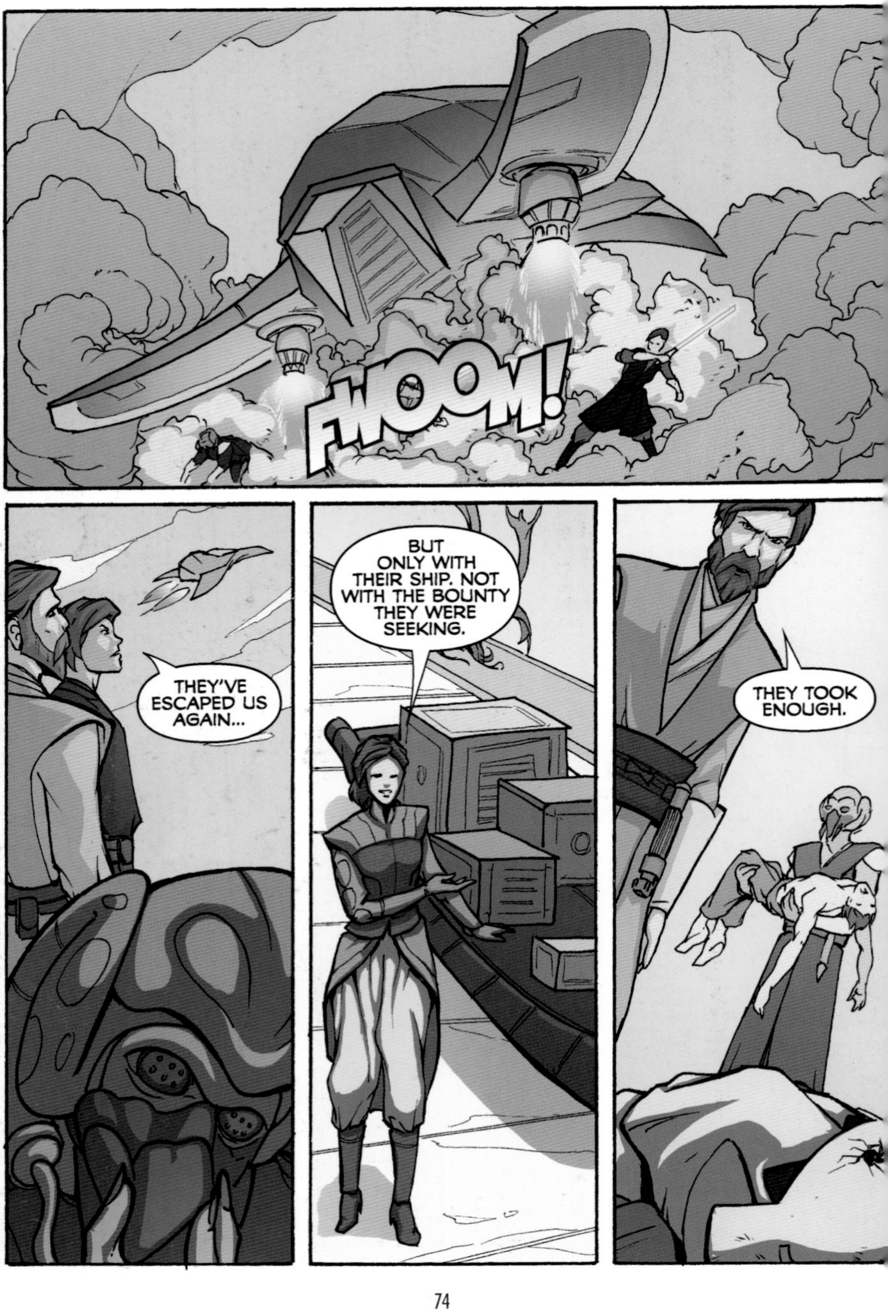
FWOOM!
THEY'VE ESCAPED US AGAIN...
BUT ONLY WITH THEIR SHIP. NOT WITH THE BOUNTY THEY WERE SEEKING.
THEY TOOK ENOUGH.

THE END

WITH THANKS TO DAVE FILONI AND KATIE LUCAS

STAR WARS GRAPHIC NOVEL TIMELINE (IN YEARS)

Omnibus: Tales of the Jedi—5,000–3,986 BSW4

Knights of the Old Republic—3,964–3,963 BSW4

The Old Republic—3653, 3678 BSW4

Knight Errant—1,032 BSW4

Jedi vs. Sith—1,000 BSW4

Omnibus: Rise of the Sith—33 BSW4

Episode I: The Phantom Menace—32 BSW4

Omnibus: Emissaries and Assassins—32 BSW4

Omnibus: Quinlan Vos—Jedi in Darkness—31–30 BSW4

Omnibus: Menace Revealed—31–22 BSW4

Honor and Duty—22 BSW4

Blood Ties—22 BSW4

Episode II: Attack of the Clones—22 BSW4

Clone Wars—22–19 BSW4

Clone Wars Adventures—22–19 BSW4

General Grievous—22–19 BSW4

Episode III: Revenge of the Sith—19 BSW4

Dark Times—19 BSW4

Omnibus: Droids—5.5 BSW4

Omnibus: Boba Fett—3 BSW4–10 ASW4

Omnibus: At War with the Empire—1 BSW4

Episode IV: A New Hope—SW4

Classic Star Wars—0–3 ASW4

Omnibus: A Long Time Ago . . .—0–4 ASW4

Empire—0 ASW4

Omnibus: The Other Sons of Tatooine—0 ASW4

Omnibus: Early Victories—0–3 ASW4

Jabba the Hutt: The Art of the Deal—1 ASW4

Episode V: The Empire Strikes Back—3 ASW4

Omnibus: Shadows of the Empire—3.5–4.5 ASW4

Episode VI: Return of the Jedi—4 ASW4

Omnibus: X-Wing Rogue Squadron—4–5 ASW4

Heir to the Empire—9 ASW4

Dark Force Rising—9 ASW4

The Last Command—9 ASW4

Dark Empire—10 ASW4

Crimson Empire—11 ASW4

Jedi Academy: Leviathan—12 ASW4

Union—19 ASW4

Chewbacca—25 ASW4

Invasion—25 ASW4

Legacy—130–137 ASW4

Old Republic Era
25,000 – 1000 years before
Star Wars: A New Hope

Rise of the Empire Era
1000 – 0 years before
Star Wars: A New Hope

Rebellion Era
0 – 5 years after
Star Wars: A New Hope

New Republic Era
5 – 25 years after
Star Wars: A New Hope

New Jedi Order Era
25+ years after
Star Wars: A New Hope

Legacy Era
130+ years after
Star Wars: A New Hope

Vector
Crosses four eras in the timeline

Volume 1 contains:
Knights of the Old Republic Volume 5
Dark Times Volume 3

Volume 2 contains:
Rebellion Volume 4
Legacy Volume 6

BSW4 = before *Episode IV: A New Hope*. ASW4 = after *Episode IV: A New Hope*.

FOR MORE ADVENTURE IN A GALAXY FAR, FAR, AWAY . . .

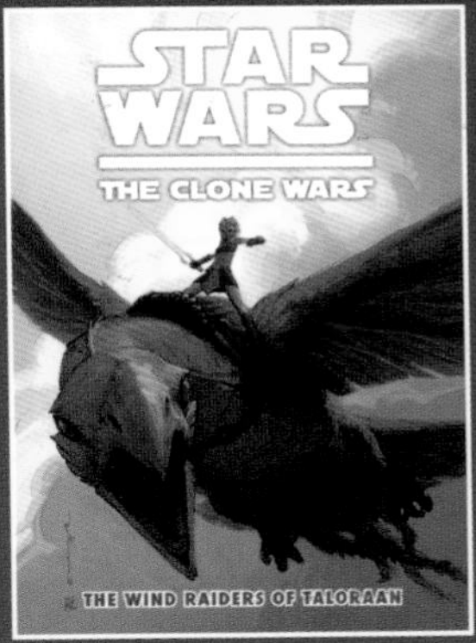
STAR WARS
THE CLONE WARS
THE WIND RAIDERS OF TALORAAN

STAR WARS: THE CLONE WARS—THE WIND RAIDERS OF TALORAAN
978-1-59582-231-4 | $7.99

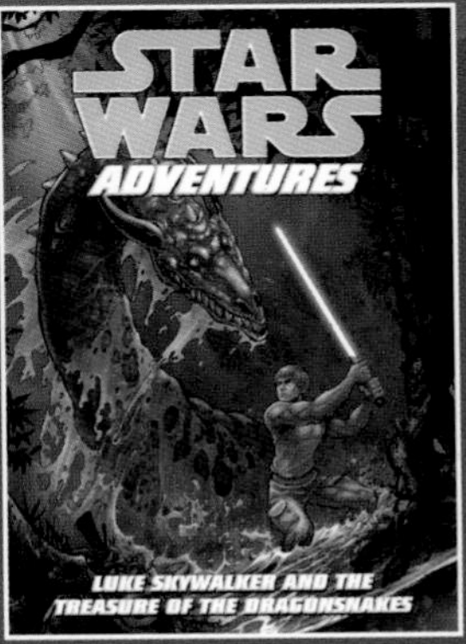
STAR WARS
ADVENTURES
LUKE SKYWALKER AND THE TREASURE OF THE DRAGONSNAKES

STAR WARS ADVENTURES: LUKE SKYWALKER AND THE TREASURE OF THE DRAGONSNAKES
978-1-59582-347-2 | $7.99

STAR WARS ADVENTURES: HAN SOLO AND THE HOLLOW MOON OF KHORYA
978-1-59582-198-0 | $7.99

STAR WARS ADVENTURES: PRINCESS LEIA AND THE ROYAL RANSOM
978-1-59582-147-8 | $7.99

STAR WARS ADVENTURES: THE WILL OF DARTH VADER
978-1-59582-435-6 | $7.99

STAR WARS ADVENTURES: BOBA FETT AND THE SHIP OF FEAR
978-1-59582-436-3 | $7.99

STAR WARS: THE CLONE WARS—SHIPYARDS OF DOOM
978-1-59582-207-9 | $7.99

STAR WARS: THE CLONE WARS—CRASH COURSE
978-1-59582-230-7 | $7.99

STAR WARS: THE CLONE WARS—SLAVES OF THE REPUBLIC
978-1-59582-349-6 | $9.99

STAR WARS: THE CLONE WARS—THE COLOSSUS OF DESTINY
978-1-59582-416-5 | $7.99

STAR WARS: THE CLONE WARS—IN SERVICE OF THE REPUBLIC
978-1-59582-487-5 | $7.99

STAR WARS: THE CLONE WARS—HERO OF THE CONFEDERACY
978-1-59582-552-0 | $7.99

STAR WARS: THE CLONE WARS—DEADLY HANDS OF SHON-JU
978-1-59582-545-2 | $7.99

STAR WARS: THE CLONE WARS—THE ENEMY WITHIN
978-1-59582-845-3 | $7.99

STAR WARS: THE CLONE WARS—THE SITH HUNTERS
978-1-59582-949-8 | $7.99

AVAILABLE AT YOUR LOCAL COMICS SHOP OR BOOKSTORE

To find a comics shop in your area, call 1-888-266-4226
For more information or to order direct: • On the web: darkhorse.com • E-mail: mailorder@darkhorse.com
Phone: 1-800-862-0052 Mon.–Fri. 9 AM to 5 PM Pacific Time.

DARK HORSE BOOKS
darkhorse.com

STAR WARS
CLONE WARS
ADVENTURES

Don't miss any of the action-packed adventures of your favorite **STAR WARS**® characters, available at comics shops and bookstores in a galaxy near you!

$6.99 each!

Volume 1	**Volume 2**	**Volume 3**	**Volume 4**	**Volume 5**
ISBN 978-1-59307-243-8	ISBN 978-1-59307-271-1	ISBN 978-1-59307-307-7	ISBN 978-1-59307-402-9	ISBN 978-1-59307-483-

Volume 6	**Volume 7**	**Volume 8**	**Volume 9**	**Volume 10**
ISBN 978-1-59307-567-5	ISBN 978-1-59307-678-8	ISBN 978-1-59307-680-1	ISBN 978-1-59307-832-4	ISBN 978-1-59307-878-